ReADiNG BASeBall

Barbara Gregorich and Christopher Jennison

Illustrated by Doug Klauba

Good Year Books

An Imprint of Scott Foresman / Addison Wesley
A Divison of Addison Wesley Longman

Dedication

For Fred Schuld: teacher, baseball fan, friend. BG

For my brother Nick, the top of his class. CJ

Good Year Books are available for most basic curriculum subjects plus many enrichment areas. For more Good Year Books, contact your local bookseller or educational dealer. For a complete catalog with information about other Good Year Books, please write:

> **Good Year Books**
> **Scott Foresman**
> **1900 East Lake Avenue**
> **Glenview, IL 60025**

Design by Karen Kohn & Associates, Ltd.
Copyright © 1997 Barbara Gregorich and Christopher Jennison.
All Rights Reserved.
Printed in the United States of America.

ISBN 0-673-36307-4

1 2 3 4 5 6 7 8 9 - MH - 04 03 02 01 00 99 98 97 96

Preface

Motivation is one of the keys to a successful learning experience, and the motivation inherent in an activity with a baseball connection should prove to be potent. Researchers agree. A study supported by the Alfred P. Sloan Foundation found that sixth graders prefer involvements that combine work and play. John Dewey predicted such a finding years earlier when he wrote, ". . . experience is most rewarding when it involves the seemingly contradictory traits of rigor and playfulness."

When it comes to baseball, all young fans enjoy following the careers of contemporary superstars such as Frank Thomas, Greg Maddux, Carlos Baerga, and Ken Griffey, Jr. But the depth of baseball's appeal goes beyond the immediate. Of all the major sports, its roots go back the furthest. And it is the only sport that offers a rich body of literature. Statistical, juvenile, fiction, and nonfiction books, analysis; instructional literature; stage plays; screenplays; and poems celebrate the game's many moods and colors.

The activities included in *Reading Baseball* are meant to challenge, as well as entertain. The forty-eight selections include fiction and nonfiction describing baseball from the late nineteenth century to today. They cover biographies, history, reporting, how-to, letters to the editor, poetry, and more. Assignments based on these readings range from one-page skill reviews to more lengthy projects. Throughout, activities integrate reading, writing, listening, and speaking skills in an authentic context. In *Teaching PreK–8,* Maryann and Gary Manning assert that "the language arts are best learned naturally as students engage in these processes in authentic ways using whole and real-life activities and materials; and reading and writing are both social activities and are best learned through interaction with others." *Reading Baseball* supplies the tools to provide just this kind of learning experience.

The book is divided into two sections and can be used in a variety of ways. Activities on reproducible pages in the first part can be assigned to individual students, while the Projects in the second part can be completed individually or by small or large groups of students working cooperatively. The entire book might become the central resource in a learning center on baseball, or provide the basis for a cross-curricular unit on baseball. The assignments can be used for review, reinforcement, and enrichment. Your students are sure to love a chance to stage a "performance" of "Casey at the Bat." Some will enjoy writing an imaginary scouting report, while others will find a research project on early team uniforms engrossing. A writer's workshop could develop readily from a reporting assignment, a screenplay, or a history of baseball nicknames. And a few projects will challenge your students to write their own stories and poems.

Preface

And don't hesitate to assign these exercises to girls. The next time you go to a ball game, or watch one on television, notice how many girls are attending. Little League play now includes girls, and they play softball and baseball at many levels of competition. Several readings in the book deal with the All-American Girls Baseball League, an organization celebrated in the movie, *A League of Their Own.*

Although the grade range of the book is fourth through eighth, no levels are assigned to specific activities. Abilities and aptitudes can vary widely from grade to grade, as well as within grade levels. A professional teacher is the best judge, finally, of an activity's appropriateness.

The authors of this book hope you will derive as much enjoyment from it as your students will. As Dewey proposed, rigor and playfulness need not be contradictory.

Contents

PAGE	Activities
2	Roberto Clemente
4	As He Sees Them
6	Take Me Out to the Ball Game
8	Rickey Henderson
10	Letters to the Editor
12	How to Play First Base
14	The Secret Life of Bats
16	The Negro Leagues Book
18	It's a Hit
20	Overdog
22	A League of Their Own
24	What If?
26	Rabid Fans
28	Slants, Whiffs, Safeties
30	Visualize Yourself
32	Interview with Nellie M. Kearns
34	The Baseball
36	Baseball's Treasure Trove
38	Pride Goeth
40	Classic vs. Modern
42	Martin Dihigo
44	How to Be a Person First
46	Humongous Trivia

From *Reading Baseball*, published by Good Year Books. Copyright © 1997 Barbara Gregorich and Christopher Jennison.

Contents

From *Reading Baseball*, published by Good Year Books. Copyright © 1997 Barbara Gregorich and Christopher Jennison.

PAGE	Projects
52	Best Dressed
54	Two Haiku
56	The Spark That Lit the Fire
58	You Can't Play in Skirts
60	A Day at the Ballpark
62	Fantasy Baseball
64	The Detroit Tigers
68	Careers in Baseball
70	Casey at the Bat
74	Earth and Sky
76	Sea Dogs and Snappers
78	Third-Base Belle
80	Caught in a Draft
82	Hooray for Hoy!
84	Instruction
86	Big: As in Unit, As in Hurt
88	The Long Search
90	Native American Players
92	Letter of Resignation
94	From Hand to Heart
96	Haiku for the Seasons
98	The Box Score
102	The Atlanta Braves
106	The Curse of the Billy Goat
110	The Gift of Beisu Boru
115	Answer Key

 **Activities**

Roberto Clemente

"Do not worry," Roberto Clemente told his teammates at the start of the 1971 World Series. "I will carry the team." Clemente was speaking to the young and inexperienced members of the Pittsburgh Pirates who had World Series jitters. He was telling them that he, a veteran with seventeen years of play and the 1960 World Series victory behind him, would take responsibility. This allowed his teammates to relax.

Clemente kept his word, and his young teammates relaxed enough to win the 1971 World Series against the Baltimore Orioles, four games to three. Roberto hit homers in the sixth and seventh games, batting a tremendous .414 and fielding spectacularly. He was chosen the World Series Most Valuable Player.

A native of Puerto Rico, Clemente was a selfless and heroic ballplayer who also happened to be a selfless and heroic man. On December 31, 1972, those who did not already know this learned the truth when they heard the devastating news of his death. On New Year's Eve, as millions celebrated, Roberto Clemente was flying critically needed food and medical supplies to Nicaragua, which had just been hit by a shattering earthquake. His plane crashed, and the world lost a hero.

According to the rules of the National Baseball Hall of Fame in Cooperstown, New York, a player must be retired from baseball or dead for at least five years before he becomes eligible for election to the Hall. In 1973, the Hall waived these requirements for Clemente and inducted its first Latino player.

"Don't worry," veteran Willie Stargell told his young Pirate teammates at the start of the 1979 World Series. "I'll carry the team." Stargell did, setting a Series record for extra-base hits and leading the Pirates to a World Series victory over (once again) the Baltimore Orioles.

Roberto Clemente set an example his teammates—and the world—would never forget.

Activities

A *fact* is something that has happened or can be proved true. An *opinion* is a belief or attitude. Read each statement below. Write *F* if it states a fact; write *O* if it states an opinion.

_____ **1.** Clemente batted .414 in the 1971 World Series.

_____ **2.** Roberto Clemente was a selfless and heroic man.

_____ **3.** Willie Stargell probably learned a lot from Clemente.

_____ **4.** The rules of the Baseball Hall of Fame state that a player must be retired from baseball or dead for at least five years before he becomes eligible for election to the Hall.

_____ **5.** The Pittsburgh Pirates won the World Series in 1960, 1971, and 1979.

_____ **6.** Clemente died when his plane crashed.

7. The title of this article is a "fact" title. Write a new title that is an "opinion" title.

_____

8. Write two sentences that express your opinion of Roberto Clemente.

_____

_____

As He Sees Them

An umpire is supposed to call each pitch and each play and each situation as he sees it. "Call 'em as he sees 'em" means that an umpire must be absolutely honest and aboveboard. Long ago, an umpire in the Negro Leagues in Texas made sure that he "saw 'em" from the best possible angle.

If a runner was going to slide, the umpire ran alongside him and slid at the same time! Then, lying on the ground, the umpire made his call so that the fans could see it. If he raised his hand, the runner was safe. If he raised his foot, the runner was out. Sometimes a runner would over-slide, then try to scramble back to the bag before the baseman tagged him. In such cases, the umpire would raise first a foot, then a hand, then a foot

(or vice versa), correcting his call as the situation changed. Imagine what fun the crowd had watching the umpire do a belly flop and then thrash his hands and feet around.

This Texas Negro Leagues umpire was quite an entertainer in other ways, too. Instead of yelling, "Y'er out!" to indicate that the batter was out, he would shout, "Batter *dis-ap-point*-ed!" If the batter earned a base on balls, the umpire would announce, "Reward for patience is yours, mister." Or sometimes he would say, "Pitcher in the wrong alley for the fourth time."

One thing is certain: fans must have enjoyed seeing this umpire as much as they enjoyed seeing the players.

From *Reading Baseball*, published by Good Year Books. Copyright © 1997 Barbara Gregorich and Christopher Jennison.

NAME _____   DATE _____

Activities

Read each set of sentences. Number the sentences 1, 2, 3 in the order the events would happen.

A. _____   Umpire shouts, "Pitcher in the wrong alley for the fourth time."
   _____   Pitcher throws ball three.
   _____   Pitcher throws last pitch to this batter.

B. _____   Runner breaks from first base to steal second base.
   _____   Umpire rushes from plate to second base.
   _____   Runner and umpire slide.

C. _____   Umpire judges pitch to be third strike.
   _____   Umpire says, "Batter *dis-ap-point*-ed!"
   _____   Umpire announces, "Play ball!"

D. _____   Umpire, lying on the ground, raises his hand.
   _____   Runner, still in motion, overshoots the bag and umpire raises foot.
   _____   Runner slides into second base before he is tagged.

E. Write a new title for this article. The new title should hint at the order in which things happen. _____

F. Imagine that you are an umpire. Write your own calls for each situation:

Batter swings and misses, third strike. _____
Batter is hit by pitch, gets to go to first base. _____
Runner tries to steal home, is tagged out. _____

Take Me Out to the Ball Game

In 1908 Jack Norworth wrote the words to "Take Me Out to the Ballgame" in fifteen minutes while riding on public transportation. His friend Albert Von Tilzer composed the music.

Nelly Kelly loved baseball games,
Knew the players, knew all their
    names,
You could see her there ev'ry day,
Shout "Hurray," when they'd play.
Her boy friend by the name of Joe
Said, "To Coney Isle, dear, let's go,"
Then Nelly started to fret and pout,
And to him I heard her shout.

"Take me out to the ball game,
Take me out with the crowd,
Buy me some peanuts and
    Cracker Jack,
I don't care if I never get back.

Let me root root root for the
    home team,
If they don't win it's a shame,
For it's one two three strikes, you're out
At the old ball game."

Nelly Kelly was sure some fan,
She would root just like any man,
Told the umpire he was wrong,
All along, good and strong.
When the score was just two to two,
Nelly Kelly knew what to do,
Just to cheer up the boys she knew,
She made the gang sing this song.

(REPEAT CHORUS)

—Jack Norworth

From *Reading Baseball*, published by Good Year Books. Copyright © 1997 Barbara Gregorich and Christopher Jennison.

Activities

Answer each question below.

1. Where does Nelly Kelly's boyfriend want to go?

_____

2. How is this a clue that Nelly Kelly lives in New York City? _____

_____

3. The words to a popular song are called *lyrics,* and the person who writes them is called *a lyricist.* The lyricist of "Take Me Out to the Ballgame" is

_____.

4. The chorus of this song begins with the line, _____.

5. The words of the chorus are spoken by _____.

6. Poets and songwriters sometimes want to shorten a word by one syllable so that the number of syllables in certain lines is the same. A poet might write *whate'er* (what ER) instead of *whatever* (what EV er) because the shortened word has two syllables instead of three. Such a shortened word is called an *elision.* What is the elision in the first stanza of "Take Me Out to the Ball Game"?

_____

7. Back in 1908, the full word for which Norworth wrote an elision must have been pronounced with _____ syllables. Today, we pronounce it with _____ syllables.

8. In two sentences, explain why you like or dislike this song. _____

_____

_____

Rickey Henderson

Rickey Henderson was born in Chicago, but nobody associates him with that city. Some people associate him with New York City, where from 1985–1989 he played for the Yankees, scoring a league-leading 146 runs in 1985 and another league-leading 130 runs the following year. In addition, while a Yankee, Henderson led the league in stolen bases three of his five seasons.

However, despite his Yankee glory years, most people associate Henderson with Oakland. There he played his rookie year, 1979, stealing an attention-getting 33 bases in 89 games. A mere three years later, in 1982, Henderson swiped a phenomenal 130 bases in a single season, breaking Lou Brock's single-season record. Along the way, he led the league in other statistics, including most runs, most hits, and most bases on balls. In 1985 the Athletics traded Henderson to the Yankees, but in 1989, when injuries slowed him down, the Yankees traded him back. It is with the Oakland A's that he will always be associated.

No matter which city fans think of when they think of Henderson, they are thinking of the most powerful leadoff man in the history of baseball. If success can be judged by doing the job you are assigned to do, then Henderson ranks with the best players in history. A leadoff batter must get on base and then score runs: the "Man of Steal," as he was called, succeeded at both.

In doing his job, Henderson helped his team to enter the playoffs and World Series. In 1989 he was chosen World Series Most Valuable Player and the following year he was named the American League MVP when, in addition to scoring a league-leading 119 runs, he batted .325 and walloped 28 home runs. Again, the A's went to the World Series. The man with more stolen bases than any other player, the most powerful leadoff batter in history, Rickey Henderson will one day be associated with some place other than Oakland . . . Cooperstown, New York.

From *Reading Baseball*, published by Good Year Books. Copyright © 1997 Barbara Gregorich and Christopher Jennison.

Activities

Write **T** if a statement below is true. Write **F** if it is false.

_____ 1. Rickey Henderson played for the Athletics and the Mets.

_____ 2. He played for the A's at the beginning of his career.

_____ 3. Henderson stole more bases than Lou Brock did.

_____ 4. Batting third, Henderson hit game-winning home runs.

_____ 5. Rickey Henderson was a fast runner, but not a good hitter.

_____ 6. He played for the Blue Jays throughout the 1990s.

_____ 7. His nickname is the "Man of Steal."

_____ 8. If this story were titled "Second to None on the Base Paths," it would tell the truth.

_____ 9. The injuries that slowed Henderson down on the base paths were probably injuries to the hands and shoulders.

_____10. Henderson played in more than one World Series.

STOLEN BY
RICKEY HENDERSON

Letters to the Editor

Last week we received more than two hundred letters on the baseball strike. The ones printed below are a representative sampling.

They make millions of dollars a year. The average fan doesn't. They're supposed to be playing a game they love. Why don't they play the game for love, not money? I know hundreds of people who would play for free. They should just play baseball without squawking.

Joe Average Citizen

I'm just a kid who wants to see baseball games. My Grandma came to visit and we ordered tickets to the Orioles game. Then the players went on strike and the tickets weren't any good. Baseball is supposed to be played all summer long. It's not fair that it isn't.

Melissa, age 11

Why are fans into bashing base-ball players? Boxers make $20 million for a fight that lasts an hour . . . maybe. Singers make millions for one-night concerts. Actors make millions for six weeks' worth of filming. All these entertainers make more than even the wealthiest ballplayer. For some reason, fans really have it in for ballplayers. I think fans should examine their own motives for treating ballplayers much worse than they treat other entertainers. Why do they do it?

J. T. Smith

Activities

After each statement, write the name of the letter writer or writers who would agree with it.

1. Fans have a double standard: one for baseball players and another for other entertainers.

   _____

2. Baseball players should just play ball and not go on strike.

   _____

3. It is unfair to baseball fans when the players go on strike.

   _____

4. People who make millions should not complain about how they are treated.

   _____

5. Players owe it to fans to play all season long. _____

6. Fans don't mind if a movie star makes $12 million in six weeks, but they get very upset if a baseball player makes $4 million in thirty weeks.

   _____

7. Kids don't want to understand why the players are on strike. Kids just want to see baseball games.

   _____

8. People who get to do what they love should do it for free.

   _____

9. Write your own "Letter to the Editor" about the baseball strike.

How to Play First Base

As a first baseman you will play either in, deep, or halfway, depending on what's happening in the game. When you definitely expect a bunt, play in to field the ball as quickly as possible. If an extra-base hit would allow a runner to score, play deep to guard the foul line. Play deep when a strong left-handed hitter comes to bat. Play halfway and to the right when a right-hander hits.

Learn to use one hand when playing first. Catch the ball in the glove, and use that hand to tag the runner. When practicing, try putting your throwing hand in your back pocket. One-hand confidence will make you a swifter, surer fielder.

Stretch to receive the throws. Taking the throw far in front of you, with your foot on the bag, puts time on your side. The ball reaches your glove faster.

Use your body at first base to block bad throws. Don't let a ball get past you, allowing runners to take an extra base or score. Knock down any ground ball. Fall on your knees to stop it, or throw yourself full-length in front of it. The bag is so close that you can pick up the ball and make the play even from a down position.

When holding a runner on first, hold your glove out for the pickoff play. This gives the pitcher a good target. Try to stay in fair territory when holding a runner on. As soon as the pitcher throws to the batter, get into your fielding position. If the runner does steal, shout, "There he goes" to the catcher. If runners on second or third try to steal, shout to the pitcher.

Keep the double play in mind. When you must throw to second base for the double play, keep your throw out of the path of the runner. Also, keep the throw on the outfield side of the bag, not the infield side.

When you are the cutoff man, don't get too close to home plate. You should receive the throw from the outfield closer to the infield edge than to home plate. Always hold your hands up high if you're the cutoff man. This gives the outfielder a good target. Listen for the catcher's directions when you're the cutoff man.

From *Reading Baseball*, published by Good Year Books. Copyright © 1997 Barbara Gregorich and Christopher Jennison.

NAME _____   DATE _____

Activities

Imagine that you are playing first base. Finish each statement below to explain why you play a certain way.

1. If you are holding a runner on first base, you should hold your glove out

   because _____.

2. You should stretch to receive throws because _____

   _____.

3. You should learn to play one-handed because _____

   _____.

4. You should block the ball with your body
   because if a ball gets past you,

   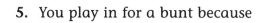

5. You play in for a bunt because

   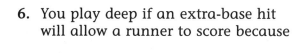

6. You play deep if an extra-base hit
   will allow a runner to score because

   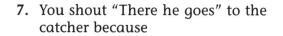

7. You shout "There he goes" to the
   catcher because

   _____.

8. If you are the cutoff man, you hold both hands up high because

   _____.

The Secret Life of Bats

aseball players seem more superstitious than other athletes. For example, a pitcher in the midst of a winning streak may insist upon wearing the same pair of unwashed "lucky socks" until the streak ends. An outfielder will avoid stepping on a foul line when he leaves the field for fear of jinxing himself. But the thing that most players are superstitious about is the care and use of their bats.

Hall-of-Fame shortstop John "Honus" Wagner of Pittsburgh believed that no bat had more than one hundred hits in it—and it might have fewer. As soon as Honus made a hundred hits with a bat, he would never use it again. In the 1960s, San Francisco Giants slugger Orlando Cepeda became convinced that each bat contained only one hit. Once Orlando got that hit, he would discard the bat. Some old-time players feared that if the bat of a great hitter like Ted Williams accidentally touched the bat of a weak hitter, hits would "leak" from the slugger's bat and be lost.

"Shoeless Joe" Jackson of the Chicago White Sox, whose .356 lifetime batting average is the third highest in history, used to transport every one of his bats to his home in South Carolina between seasons. "Bats," he said, "are like ballplayers. They hate cold weather." Babe Ruth insisted that as many of his bats as possible be made from wood speckled with pine knots, a condition that most players considered a defect. Babe was convinced it brought him luck. Hall-of-Fame outfielder "Wahoo Sam" Crawford was even fussier. He would not use a bat that he had not fashioned with his own hands.

Perhaps because wooden bats are made from something that was once living, players of all generations have felt an affection for their bats and even ascribed magic powers to them. Today only professionals use wooden bats. Because wood is so expensive, amateur teams have been using aluminum bats since the 1970s. But aluminum bats have never inspired the attachment that wood does—nor the superstitions.

From *Reading Baseball*, published by Good Year Books. Copyright © 1997 Barbara Gregorich and Christopher Jennison.

Reprinted with permission of William Curran, who is also author of *Strikeout: A Celebration of the Art of Pitching* (New York: Crown Publishers, 1995).

ActiviTies

Write each vocabulary word from the story about bats next to its definition.

_____   1. to move from one place to another

_____   2. to fill with emotion

_____   3. to bring bad luck to

_____   4. the middle position or part

_____   5. to throw away

_____   6. dotted or flecked

_____   7. an imperfection

_____   8. requiring great attention to details

_____   9. to persuade

_____   10. to make or shape

_____   11. a tender feeling toward; love

_____   12. an irrational belief that one thing not related to another causes it

INSPIRE SPECKLED CONVINCE DISCARD FUSSY AFFECTION TRANSPORT FASHION MIDST SUPERSTITION JINX DEFECT

The Negro Leagues Book

Edited by Dick Clark and Larry Lester

A Monumental Work from the Negro Leagues Committee of The Society for American Baseball Research

Contents

Key to Abbreviations	11
The Negro Leagues: A Brief History by Merl Kleinknecht	15
Great Teams	20
Teams and Their Cities	30
Hall of Fame Players by Larry Lester	33
Rosters	51
Standings, 1920–1955	159
Register	167
Seasonal Leaders	238
East-West All-Star Games, 1933–1950	242
From the Negro Leagues to the Majors	255
Organized Baseball Records	261
Bibliography	337
Newspapers and Sports Writers	371
Reference Books	377
Theses and Dissertations	379
Black Stars on the Silver Screen	381

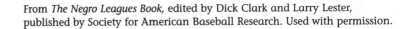

From *The Negro Leagues Book*, edited by Dick Clark and Larry Lester, published by Society for American Baseball Research. Used with permission.

ActiviTies

To which page would you turn to look up information on each topic below?
Write the correct page number on each line.

_____ 1. Which players participated in the 1939
            All-Star Game?

_____ 2. Was George W. Stovey on the 1888
            Cuban Giants team?

_____ 3. Is there a film about the Negro Leagues
            entitled *Kings on the Hill?*

_____ 4. Who were some of the African American
            sportswriters during the Negro Leagues
            era?

_____ 5. What do SLCB and NNL stand for?

_____ 6. Did the Baltimore Elite Giants finish ahead
            of the Homestead Grays in 1942?

_____ 7. How many major league ballplayers
            also played in the Negro Leagues, and
            who were they?

_____ 8. Are Judy Johnson, Pop Lloyd, and Satchel Paige in the National
            Baseball Hall of Fame?

_____ 9. What were the Negro Leagues, how long did they last, and who
            were some of the players?

_____ 10. What were the names of all the players who ever played in the
            Negro Leagues?

It's A Hit

There's a big difference between hitting the baseball and getting a hit. "He hit the ball" is not necessarily the same as "He got a hit."

Is it difficult to hit a baseball? Ted Williams, perhaps the greatest hitter in the history of the game, said that hitting a speeding baseball with a rounded stick was the single most difficult feat in all of sports. Yes—it is difficult to hit a baseball. It's difficult because the pitcher has more advantages than the batter. The pitcher stands elevated on a mound and hurls the ball down at the batter. The pitcher knows what he's going to throw. The batter has to guess at what the pitcher will throw (fastball? curve? change of pace?). It's difficult because the batter must make the all-important decision of whether to swing and where to swing in a fraction of a second. A ball traveling toward the plate at more than eighty miles an hour arrives at the plate in less than half a second.

But let's say that the batter does connect. The fans hear the loud and satisfying smack of wood hitting leather. All eyes watch the ball as it travels back in the direction from which it came. No doubt about it, the batter has hit the ball. But the chances that the batter has made a hit are even less than the chances that he could hit the ball in the first place! Behind the pitcher stand seven other players, each ready to catch the ball before it touches the ground, or to catch the ball on the hop, throw to a baseman, and put the batter out. When either of these things happens, the batter has not gotten a hit. The secret of getting hits, said "Wee Willie" Keeler, champion batter of the nineteenth century, is to "hit 'em where they ain't." When a batter hits the ball where nobody can field it in time, the batter is usually credited with a hit.

How difficult is it to get a hit? An average player has a fielding percentage of .960 or higher. A good runner is successful approximately 75 percent of the time when attempting to steal a base. A good pitcher has a winning percentage above .500. But a good hitter? A good hitter hits only slightly above .300. The highest lifetime batting average in history belongs to Ty Cobb, who hit .366. Hitting is so difficult that when you succeed three times out of ten, you're fantastic.

ACTIVITIES

A *summary* is a shortened version of an article or speech. Read each summary below. Only one of the summaries accurately reflects the contents of the article. Answer the questions that follow.

A. Every time a batter hits the ball, the scorekeeper does not necessarily record it as a hit. If a batter sacrifices (bunts, or hits a long fly to the outfield) to drive in a run, hitting the ball does not count as a hit. In fact, it doesn't even count as an at-bat!

B. Hitting a baseball is very difficult. The batter has to guess what is coming and react quickly. But even if the batter hits the ball, the effort is not necessarily counted as a hit. A fielder can catch the ball on the fly or throw the batter out at one of the bases. If a batter hits a ball that can't be successfully fielded, he is usually given credit for a hit.

C. A baseball player batting over .300 is a successful player because it is very difficult to hit a baseball traveling more than eighty miles an hour. Batters have less than half a second from the time the ball leaves the pitcher's hand until it arrives at the plate. They must decide whether to swing and where to swing. If the batter hits a ball that nobody catches, it's a hit.

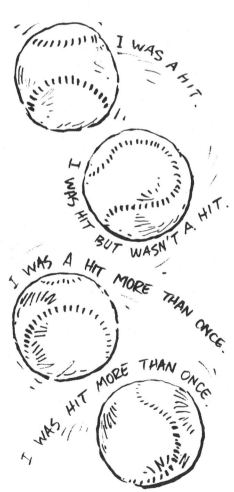

_____ is not the best summary because

_____

_____

_____ is not the best summary because

_____

_____

_____is the most accurate summary because

_____

_____

OVErdOG

Overdog Johnson is a guy
who always wins
but hardly tries.

Pitcher sails it.
Johnson nails it.
Whack!
Homerun!

Pitcher steams it.
Johnson creams it.
Thwack!
Homerun!

Pitcher smokes it.
Johnson pokes it.
Smack!
Homerun!

Pitcher fires it.
Johnson wires it.
Crack!
Ho-hum.
      —Tony Johnston

From *Reading Baseball*, published by Good Year Books. Copyright © 1997 Barbara Gregorich and Christopher Jennison.

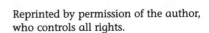

Activities

Read each sentence below. Circle the correct word or words to complete each sentence.

1. The poem is written from the point of view of the (**pitcher, batter, fan**).

2. The author calls Johnson an "overdog" to contrast him to (**doggone, underdog, top dog**).

3. A slang expression for "hits it hard" is (**fires it, creams it, whiffs**).

4. Johnson is the (**pitcher, batter, fan**).

5. A slang expression for "pitches hard and fast" is (**smokes it, nails it, boots it**).

6. The first verse of the poem sums up the author's attitude toward (**athletes in general, athletes who struggle to win, athletes for whom everything is easy**).

7. The author reveals his attitude toward such athletes in the words (**Whack! Homerun! Ho-hum**).

8. How do you feel about "overdogs"? Write several sentences that tell why you agree or disagree with the author of the poem.

   _____

   _____

   _____

9. Draw a cartoon-type illustration of "Overdog Johnson" at the plate.

A League of Their Own

Director: Penny Marshall
Cast: Tom Hanks, Geena Davis, Lori Petty,
Madonna, Rosie O'Donnell 1992

Can two baseball-loving sisters from the Pacific Northwest find happiness playing professional baseball? Can Penny Marshall, star of television sitcoms and director of the marvelous *Big,* make a film that handles women playing baseball with the respect the subject deserves? The answer to the first question is, "One can"; the answer to the second a loud "Yes."

A League of Their Own deals with a topic few Americans know anything about: the All-American Girls Baseball League. Geena Davis and Lori Petty play sisters, the former a catcher, the latter a pitcher. Davis is married, her husband fighting in World War II. Petty is single. Davis plays a "natural," talented at hitting and catching. She is strong, sure, and calm. Younger sister Petty, a better-than-average pitcher, fails at the plate, where she over-eagerly swings at pitches she should let go by, unable to hit the payoff pitches. Although she plays the role with a sometimes-grating whine, Petty represents the dedicated ballplayer—one who wants only to play baseball. In the end, this difference between the sisters directs their paths through life.

Madonna and Rosie O'Donnell provide comic relief while turning in convincing baseball scenes. But it's Tom Hanks who steals the show. A boozer, the major leaguer is washed up before his time. Given the job of managing a bunch of women who play baseball while wearing short skirts, Hanks takes the salary and does nothing. He would manage *real* ballplayers, but he doesn't consider the women real ballplayers. The women show him otherwise—that we *all* have a field of dreams—and when Hanks finally sees past the silly skirts and into the hearts of the players, he becomes a major leaguer in the full sense of the term.

From *Reading Baseball,* published by Good Year Books. Copyright © 1997 Barbara Gregorich and Christopher Jennison.

ActiviTies

Movie critics provide readers with opinions about movies. Read each statement below. Write **Yes** on the line if a sentence correctly expresses the author's opinion. Write **No** if a sentence does not express her opinion.

_____ 1. *Big* was a wonderful movie, and Penny Marshall did a good job of directing it.

_____ 2. The character that Lori Petty plays whines a lot, and this makes the movie more enjoyable.

_____ 3. Madonna does not do a good job of acting in this film.

_____ 4. The character played by Tom Hanks is the most interesting and attention-getting character in the film.

_____ 5. People who act in television sitcoms might not be the best people to make movies about serious subjects.

_____ 6. Geena Davis plays a character who is a naturally talented athlete.

_____ 7. The character played by Tom Hanks changes in the movie.

_____ 8. A major leaguer is a person who sees how silly it is to play baseball while wearing a skirt.

_____ 9. All people have dreams of excelling at what they love to do.

_____ 10. There is such a thing as major league behavior.

11. If you have seen *A League of Their Own,* write your own review of the movie. If you have not seen the film, write your own review of any baseball film you have seen.

What If?

Perhaps we take our national pastime for granted. Perhaps we never ask ourselves whether it—and we—have taken the best route possible. So let's indulge in a little speculation this week, a little "what iffing."

• What if the rule of 1873 that prohibited players from catching the ball in their caps never went into effect? Think about it. Perhaps those pre-1873 players whose antics apparently led to this rule knew a good thing when they did it. Just imagine—catching the ball in their caps! Think of today's huge outfield gloves. I mean, *huge!* Huge spread, huge webs for snagging the ball. If that old 1873 rule had never been put into the official baseball book of rules, perhaps players would wear little bitty gloves and huge caps! Perhaps we'd see Ken Griffey, Jr., wearing something that looks like an oversized butterfly net, running down a long fly ball that looks like a sure homer. Racing the ball toward the fence Junior sweeps off his gigantic cap, leaps into the air, thrusts the cap over the fence, and . . . Ta-da! . . . retrieves the ball and displays it to the umpire, who in a dramatic gesture declares the batter out.

• What if the rule of 1884, in which it took three strikes for an out but six balls for a walk, was never changed? You wanna know what if?

Yaawwwwnn. That's what if. Baseball today is slow enough when it takes four balls to reach first base. Increase that by 50 percent and we'd all be up until 2:00 A.M. to watch the end of a game that started at 7:30 P.M. No thanks on this one.

• The rule of 1875 allowed bats to be flat on one side. That's something to think about, isn't it? Would hitting the ball be less difficult with a flat-sided bat? Would baseball have evolved into something like golf? Or does that round sphere traveling toward the batter at upwards of eighty miles per hour have affinity only for a rounded stick?

• Here's another what if. In 1928 the minor leagues of the American Association used yellow baseballs in a game. In the 1970s Charles O. Finley (the man who put polyester uniforms of yellow, green, and white on his players—but that's another what if), owner of the Oakland A's, wanted to try yellow baseballs. Or chartreuse, I forget which. The point is, what if baseballs weren't white?

What if? Think about it.

From *Reading Baseball*, published by Good Year Books. Copyright © 1997 Barbara Gregorich and Christopher Jennison.

ACTIVITIES

Explain how baseball would be different for each of the "what ifs?" listed below.

1. How might baseball be different if bats were flat-sided?

_____

_____

2. How might baseball be different if players still wore the baggy gray or white flannel uniforms of fifty years ago?

_____

_____

3. What if baseballs were orange or chartreuse or yellow? How would the game be different?

_____

_____

4. During the first few decades of baseball, the batter told the pitcher what kind of pitch he wanted and where he wanted it. What if this were still true?

_____

_____

_____

5. What if baseball had never been segregated, and African American ballplayers had played in the major leagues from 1869 until now. How would the game be different?

_____

_____

_____

From *Reading Baseball*, published by Good Year Books. Copyright © 1997 Barbara Gregorich and Christopher Jennison.

Rabid Fans

Emil Pietrangeli of Kenosha, Wisconsin, umpired semipro baseball for many years. When Philip K. Wrigley, owner of the Chicago Cubs, formed the All-American Girls Baseball League (AAGBL) in the 1940s, Pietrangeli was invited to umpire in the League. At first he wasn't interested because he thought the women couldn't play serious baseball. Then he went to see them play and was quite impressed. So he took the job of umpire, using the name Emil Piet.

The man in blue remembers the AAGBL as having "the best professionalism I've ever seen. . . . It was all there: the balls, bats, batboys and batgirls. It was nothing like that in the men's leagues. Sometimes they didn't even have the bases there down in the semipros."

When it came to AAGBL fans, though, Pietrangeli wasn't impressed. "Homers," he calls them. "They were worse than fans for men's teams. They backed the girls wholeheartedly. I don't know why, but they were worse when it came to the girls. Most of them were older people and they were rabid."

Pietrangeli remembers umpiring at third base in Rockford during a playoff series between the Rockford Peaches and the Kenosha Comets. "Dottie Kamenshek, their favorite, had a hook slide, a way of going into third that she'd go past it with her feet and touch it with her hand. But this time she didn't hang on to the bag and I called her out. Dottie didn't say anything, but the crowd did." They booed the umpire fiercely.

When it came time to leave the stadium, Pietrangeli had to walk through an opening surrounded by the stands. The head of the local Peaches Boosters Club was standing there with her husband, who dumped five gallons of water on the man in blue, then ran away.

"They caught him and brought him to me and asked me what to do with him," says Pietrangeli. "I let him go."

From *Reading Baseball*, published by Good Year Books. Copyright © 1997 Barbara Gregorich and Christopher Jennison.

ACTIVITIES

Look at the three incidents named below. Think about each incident. Each can be thought of as a series of at least three happenings: first this happened, then this happened, then that happened. After each incident, write the three parts of the incident in correct sequential order—in the order that the things happened.

A. The Dottie Kamenshek Incident

1. _____

2. _____

3. _____

B. The "I Don't Want to Umpire Women" Incident

1. _____

2. _____

3. _____

C. The Bucket of Water Incident

1. _____

2. _____

3. _____

Study the definitions below. Each goes with a word that is used in the story. Write the letter of the correct word next to each definition.

____	1. intensely	**a.** rabid	
____	2. partly professional	**b.** fiercely	
____	3. fans who favor the home team above all	**c.** professionalism	
____	4. furious; extremely enthusiastic	**d.** impressed	
____	5. high standards or methods	**e.** homers	
____	6. strongly affected or influenced	**f.** semipro	

From *Reading Baseball*, published by Good Year Books. Copyright © 1997 Barbara Gregorich and Christopher Jennison.

Slants, Whiffs, and Safeties

The southpaw slants of Frankie Hayes blanked the Kansas City Royals last night, and the Red Sox, sparked by Frankie's mound wizardry, emerged victorious 8-0, before thirty-two thousand frantic fans at Fenway Park. Hayes's baffling serves completely stymied the Kansas City stickmen, and eleven of them whiffed before even seven frames were rung up.

Meanwhile, Frankie's mates were tearing the cover off the ball. Jarvis Fenwick, the Beantowners' second sacker, weighed in with a three-bagger and a pair of round trippers, while Elvis Cantwell, George Mix, and Phil Passen collected three safeties each.

The Red Sox showed some slick glove work as well. They turned three twin-killings and didn't commit a single miscue. Among Hayes's hurling repertoire were roundhouse breaking balls, some real heat, and once in a while a butterfly ball that twisted the Kansas City batsmen into pretzels. Frankie allowed only three free passes, and only two Kansas City runners made it to the keystone sack.

Compared to Hayes, the Kansas City moundsmen were studies in futility. No less than six harried hurlers toiled on the hill, and not one of them worked in more than two stanzas.

The Bosox victory brought down the curtain on a successful home defense. Now our boys must face a grueling journey to enemy lands and won't return to home cooking for two long weeks, sandwiched around a holiday twin bill in the Big Apple.

From *Reading Baseball*, published by Good Year Books. Copyright © 1997 Barbara Gregorich and Christopher Jennison.

NAME _____   DATE _____

ActiviTies

Many baseball writers and reporters use slang words to make their writing more colorful. *Slang* is vocabulary special to a group or profession. It is also any fresh, colorful, informal use of language. Answer the questions below.

1. Why do you think that good writers use a minimum amount of slang?

_____

_____

2. How does slang add to the enjoyment of a story?

_____

_____

_____

3. Is slang more likely to occur in speech or in writing? Explain why you think so.

_____

_____

4. Rewrite the first paragraph of "Slants, Whiffs, and Safeties" without using slang.

_____

_____

_____

5. Write a paragraph about your favorite ballplayer using as many slang expressions as you can. Exchange the paragraph with another student. Did the other student understand what you wrote? Did you understand what the other student wrote?

Visualize Yourself

Dr. Andrea paced the locker room. Twenty-five necks turned each time she did. Fifty eyes followed her progress. The Williwaws had lost their last fifteen games. They were desperate for a win, desperate for an answer.

"The answer is to visualize yourself," said Dr. Andrea. "See yourself in action. See yourself at the critical moment. Visualize the sequence of events before they happen. See yourself go through the motions. Use your mind and mental imaging to prepare your muscles for what lies ahead."

Mitch closed his eyes. He saw the tiny lead the Williwaws had going into the ninth. A baby lead. One run. He saw the flames flicker. They would grow. The fire would spread and devour his team. The lead would go up in smoke. Mitch saw himself run in from the bullpen wearing a black suit, with high rubber boots. The number on his cap was a big bold 6. Mitch dragged a heavy hose with him. He stepped on the mound. He turned the water on the opponents. He put out the fire.

Tyler breathed slowly and deeply, visualizing himself walking to the plate. The Williwaws were behind, 6-4. Bottom of the sixth. Two out. A Williwaw runner at first, another at third. Tyler saw them out there, depending on him. The runners wore dirty, grimy uniforms. Dirt on their caps. Dust on their shoes. The bases, too, were covered with grime. Tyler stepped up to bat, holding a gigantic broom. In his back pocket was a powerful spray detergent. He was ready to do the job.

Charles squirmed nervously on the bench. He didn't want to shut his eyes. He knew what he would visualize. Dr. Andrea tapped him on the shoulder. "Close your eyes, Charles," she commanded. "You can't visualize with your eyes wide open." With a sigh, Charles closed his eyes. It was the top of the ninth, Williwaws leading, 3-2. Two outs on the opponents. A runner on second. Slugger at the plate. Charles patrolled the outfield. He knew the ball would come his way. Just knew it. All he had to do was catch the ball, and the third out would be made and the Williwaws would win. But he knew he wouldn't. Against his will, the image came trotting in. He could hear the tinkle-tinkle of the bell around its neck. He could see the sharp horns on its head, the silky little beard below its chin. *Crack!* He heard the sound of the bat meeting the ball. "Baa!" he heard the image say.

From *Reading Baseball*, published by Good Year Books. Copyright © 1997 Barbara Gregorich and Christopher Jennison.

From *Reading Baseball*, published by Good Year Books. Copyright © 1997 Barbara Gregorich and Christopher Jennison.

Activities

1. If visualizing yourself works, what will happen when Mitch takes the mound?

_____

_____

2. If visualizing yourself works, what will happen when Tyler steps to the plate?

_____

_____

3. And what will happen if a long fly ball is hit toward Charles in the outfield?

_____

_____

4. Based on information in the story, explain what *a fireman* is in baseball.

_____

_____

5. Based on information in the story, explain what *a cleanup hitter* is in baseball.

_____

_____

6. Based on the story, explain what *a goat* is in baseball or other sports.

_____

_____

7. How do you visualize yourself? Write several sentences or paragraphs explaining what you see when you visualize yourself doing something.

Interview with Nellie M. Kearns

From the 1890s through the 1930s, Bloomer Girl baseball teams barnstormed across the country. Usually consisting of six women and three men, bloomer teams played against all-male teams in the towns they visited. Nellie M. Kearns played with the All Star Ranger Girls, one of the most famous of such teams, in 1933 and 1934. Below is part of an interview with Nellie Kearns.

Q: What are some of the things you remember about the ball fields?

NK: One game we played, a small creek bordered the outer edge of the outfield. A fly ball was hit to the outfield and the fielder was chasing after the ball and they both disappeared. She went over the embankment and received several bad bruises and bumps.

The most terrifying game I played with the All Star Rangers was the day when a snake was in the outfield and sliding through the grass around my feet. I kept my eyes on the snake and not the ball game, and I was so thankful when that game was over.

Q: Are there any games in particular that you remember?

NK: It was a sad day for all the team members when "Peanuts" [pitcher Beatrice Schmidt] got hit with a line drive above the eye and had to be taken to the hospital. It took several stitches to close the wound.

I remember the game we played against the Italians, a team in Connecticut. The newspaper headlines said, "'Are Our Faces Red?' Chorus Italians As They Lose to Girls, Score 6-3." A few of the Italians walked off the field crying. They were such good players, but they took us for granted and they lost.

Q: Did you miss playing after the Ranger Girls disbanded?

NK: The 1934 season wasn't as much fun as 1933. The love of baseball was drained from my body when we had to play three games in one day. When the bat hits the ball, the cracking sound tells you the ball is coming to your field, and by the sound you'll know when to get on your horse and ride because you are going to have to run fast to catch the ball. I was so tired after three games, I played off the back of my heels for a week.

Q: Did you enjoy traveling all over the country?

NK: Oh, yes. Whenever we were in a new town, we'd go for a walk down the streets. Every time we passed a fire station, I'd say, "I would love to slide down the fireman's pole in the station." After so many of these remarks, "Tex" [Mae Wines] got tired of hearing them. One day we were taking our walk, and Tex went into the station and told one of the fireman she had a player who would like to slide down the pole. The fireman took me upstairs and instructed me how to place my feet and hands on the pole, and down I went before I was ready to go down.

From *Reading Baseball*, published by Good Year Books. Copyright © 1997 Barbara Gregorich and Christopher Jennison.

From *Reading Baseball*, published by Good Year Books. Copyright © 1997 Barbara Gregorich and Christopher Jennison.

ACTIVITIES

1. Explain what "get on your horse and ride" means.

_____

_____

2. Explain what "played off the back of my heels" means.

_____

_____

3. In what way did the Italians (a baseball team) probably take the All Star Ranger Girls for granted?

_____

_____

4. Based on this interview, list five things about the lives and playing conditions of the All Star Ranger Girls that were different from the lives and playing conditions of major leaguers.

   a) _____

   b) _____

   c) _____

   d) _____

   e) _____

5. List three questions you would ask Nellie Kearns about her playing days if you were interviewing her.

   a) _____

   b) _____

   c) _____

The Baseball

I see it rise
to conquer space
like a rocket
in a race.

It hovers at
the peak of flight
almost past
my range of sight—

Then

down it dives
by air's command
to make a landing
in my hand.

—Sandra Liatsos

"The Baseball" by Sandra Liatsos.
Copyright © 1993 by Sandra Liatsos.
Used by permission of Marian Reiner
for the author.

Activities

From *Reading Baseball*, published by Good Year Books. Copyright © 1997 Barbara Gregorich and Christopher Jennison.

1. In each four-line stanza of the poem, two words rhyme. List the two words in each stanza.

First Stanza _____

Second Stanza _____

Third Stanza _____

2. Explain why the poem is stronger and more satisfying because the last word rhymes with something.

_____

_____

3. Usually the stanzas of a poem are stacked on top of one another like paragraphs: they all start at the left-hand margin. "The Baseball" looks different on the page. Explain how the shape of the poem helps get across its meaning.

_____

_____

4. List all the words in the poem that make you think of the air or flying.

_____   _____   _____

_____   _____   _____

_____   _____   _____

5. "The Baseball" is told from the point of view of the outfielder who catches the ball. Write a poem titled "The Fielder" from the point of view of the baseball.

Baseball's Treasure Trove

Imagine a library that holds nothing but baseball books, magazines, pamphlets, audiotapes, and videos—and better yet, photographs from all of baseball's history, plus scrapbooks and scorecards painstakingly tended by long-ago fans, and much more. That library exists, part of the National Baseball Hall of Fame in Cooperstown, New York.

The library's collection holds 1.9 million pieces, according to the Hall of Fame Librarian, Jim Gates. Some of the items aren't usual library fare. Among the unique objects in his care are Christy Mathewson's piano, Casey Stengel's baby picture, and a cloth blueprint lost during the building of Comiskey Park in 1909–10, unearthed eighty years later when the ballpark was razed, and reconditioned into a "big, beautiful piece of art. It's one of our treasures," says Gates.

Of the countless treasures, the one that has touched Gates the most is the letter Lou Gehrig wrote to his wife after he was diagnosed with the disease that would take his life. "It's a beautiful letter, but hard to read," Gates says. "I could only read it once; it's just so sad."

The Baseball Hall of Fame Library handles more than thirty thousand requests a year. Users include radio, TV, and newspaper journalists; writers researching fiction and nonfiction projects; tourists taking in the Hall who want to find a photo or answer a question; students "ranging from a second grader with a homework question to a graduate student working on a dissertation"; and genealogists looking up a ballplayer in the family.

This last group unintentionally gives the Hall librarians some of their hardest professional moments. "Sometimes it turns out that Uncle Joe's been lying all these years about playing in the major leagues," Gates says. When a search through the files comes up empty, "you have to let [family members] down easy."

But there are many happy moments for Gates. One of the best, he says, is when a box of donated material arrives and he doesn't know what's inside. "It's amazing what you'll find. The anticipation just before you open the box is incredible." The other most satisfying part of his work is to see the look on the faces of young people when the librarians can answer their questions. "You go home on those days feeling great."

—Rory Metcalf

From *Reading Baseball*, published by Good Year Books. Copyright © 1997 Barbara Gregorich and Christopher Jennison.

By permission of Rory Metcalf, who has written about baseball for a number of national and regional magazines.

NAME _____ DATE _____

Activities

Find the eight vocabulary words on this page. Then find each word, or a form of each word, in the story about the Hall of Fame and read again how it is used in a sentence. Write the correct word next to each definition below.

_____ 1. very carefully, with attention to detail

_____ 2. a collection of valuable things

_____ 3. a person who studies family ancestors

_____ 4. to tear down, demolish

_____ 5. to identify something (such as a disease)

_____ 6. a long paper written by a candidate for a degree in a university

_____ 7. to contribute; to give as a gift to a cause

_____ 8. an expectation

1. List three unique items in the Baseball Hall of Fame Library.

   a) _____

   b) _____

   c) _____

2. List three specific things that people might ask the Library to help them find or verify.

   a) _____

   b) _____

   c) _____

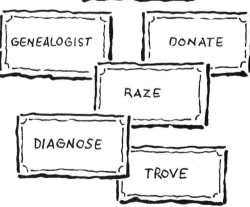

PRIDE GOETH

Bill Terry was a hard-hitting first baseman for the New York Giants who made his major league debut in 1923, at the age of twenty-five. Coming up to the majors at that age might have taught Terry some humility. But it didn't. The Giants won the pennant that year, but lost the World Series to the Yankees, four games to two.

The following season, Terry played in seventy-seven games, batting .239. The Giants won the pennant that year, too, losing the Series to the underdog Washington Senators in seven games. History's lessons were there for the taking. Or leaving.

In 1925 Terry hit his stride, playing in 133 games and batting .319. His batting average increased slowly until 1929, when he hit .372. The next year, he led the league in hits, racking up 254 of them. And his .401 average of that year made Terry the last of the .400 hitters in the National League. In 1931 he led the league in runs (121) and triples (20).

The Giants had an intense rivalry with the Brooklyn Dodgers. Both played in the same town. Both were in the National League. Both had millions of ardent fans.

In 1932, at the age of thirty-four, Bill Terry became manager of the Giants. This was quite an honor, for he succeeded the legendary John McGraw, who had managed major league baseball for thirty-three years —thirty of them with the Giants.

The following year, Terry led his team to the National League pennant and then to victory against the Senators in the World Series, four games to one. Bill Terry and the New York Giants were sitting on top of the world. In 1933 the Dodgers finished sixth, 26.5 games behind the leaders.

Early in 1934, before the season even started, Bill Terry told newsmen that the Giants would win the pennant. A reporter then asked, "Do you fear Brooklyn?" With great arrogance, Terry uttered what would become a famous line in baseball history. "Is Brooklyn still in the league?" he asked.

The year 1934 started out with the Giants winning game after game, while the Dodgers slipped down, down, down in the rankings — five games behind, ten games behind . . . fifteen . . . twenty. But the last two games of the season were between the Giants and the Dodgers. The Giants, tied with the St. Louis Cardinals for first place, needed to win both games to take the pennant. In those last two games of the 1934 season, the Dodgers defeated the Giants, not once, but twice. The Dodgers defeated the Giants not sadly, but gleefully. In 1934 the mighty fell at the feet of the lowly.

From *Reading Baseball*, published by Good Year Books. Copyright © 1997 Barbara Gregorich and Christopher Jennison.

NAME _____   DATE _____

Activities

A *summary* is a shortened version of an article or speech. Read each summary below. Only one of the summaries accurately reflects the contents of the article. Complete the statements that follow.

A. The game of baseball provided Bill Terry with clues and hints everywhere, including the fact that the heavily favored Giants lost the World Series to the underdog Washington Senators. But when Terry and the Giants finally won a World Series in 1933, he didn't heed the lessons of baseball. He insulted the lowly Brooklyn Dodgers. As a result, the Dodgers prevented the Giants from winning the pennant.

B. Bill Terry was a hard-hitting first baseman for the New York Giants. Terry was so good that, although he started out with a lowly .239 batting average, he batted over .300 very soon. In 1930 he led the league in hits. His .401 average of that year made him the last of the .400 hitters in the National League. Terry was appointed manager of the Giants, succeeding the legendary John McGraw. He led the Giants to a World Series victory.

C. You win some, you lose some. This was what Bill Terry learned during his career as first baseman for the New York Giants during the 1920s and 1930s, when he also served as manager.

_____ is the most accurate summary because _____

_____

_____

"Pride goeth before destruction, and an haughty spirit before a fall." Explain why the title of this story is taken from the proverb.

_____

_____

_____

Classic vs. Modern

Certain baseball stadiums can be called classic, others modern. Typical of the classic design was Griffith Stadium, which used to stand in Washington, D.C. Along with all but a precious few of the classics, Griffith was demolished.

Constructed in the first twenty years of the century, classic stadiums were built in cities, where people could walk to the park or take a trolley or bus. Their shapes conformed to the dimensions of existing city structures, usually bounded by four city streets, or perhaps two streets, a railroad line, and a factory building. This is why classic stadiums often had such strange shapes and dimensions. Larch Street, Howard University, a lumber mill, Georgia Avenue, and Spruce Street bounded Griffith Stadium, for example. Its center field wall zigzagged inward to avoid five houses next to it. A huge tree outside the wall hung over into the field of play.

Modern stadiums became popular in the 1950s. Many of them serve several purposes as homes to both baseball and football games and, sometimes, soccer.

Domes cover some of them. Typical of the modern ballpark is the SkyDome in Toronto. These stadiums still stand—although some baseball owners now want to tear them down and replace them with new ones that look like the classics.

The modern stadium is usually built in the middle of a huge area of land, surrounded by acres of parking spaces. Because of its isolated location, its shape can be symmetrical. Left-field and right-field distances are equal, tapering gracefully toward center field. The outfield distances vary little from one modern stadium to the next. The 328'-400'-328' dimensions of the SkyDome do not differ significantly from the 383'-400'-383' of the new Comiskey or the 375'-404'-375' of Riverfront or the 372'-400'-372' of the Oakland Coliseum.

Watching a baseball game while sitting in a classic stadium such as the now-demolished Forbes Field or the still-existent Wrigley Field is a unique experience. The field itself plays a role in the outcome of the game. Attending a game while sitting in a modern stadium is still fun, but the field dimensions play little or no role in the outcome of the game.

From *Reading Baseball*, published by Good Year Books. Copyright © 1997 Barbara Gregorich and Christopher Jennison.

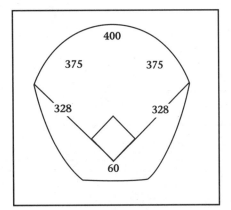

SKYDOME

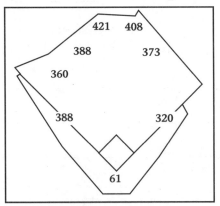

GRIFFITH STADIUM

ActiviTies

Study the diagrams and read the article. Fill in the blanks below to compare the two kinds of stadiums.

	Griffith	**SkyDome**
Type	_____	_____
Year First Occupied	_____	_____
Left Field	_____	_____
Right Field	_____	_____
Center Field	_____	_____
Describe Shape	_____	_____
Surrounded By	_____	_____

	Classic	**Modern**
Name Two of Each	_____	_____
	_____	_____
Years Built	_____	_____
Transportation To	_____	_____

Imagine yourself either a ballplayer or a baseball fan. Where would you rather play or watch baseball—in a classic stadium or a modern one? Write an essay telling why. Try to appeal to all five senses: sight, sound, touch, taste, smell.

Martin Dihigo

Martin Dihigo is the only baseball player in the world elected to three baseball halls of fame: in Cuba, Mexico, and the United States.

Born in 1906 in Cuba, Dihigo was playing professional baseball by the time he turned seventeen. An African Cuban with dark skin, he was not permitted to play in the American or National leagues, which signed only white ballplayers. And so "The Immortal," as Cubans called their hero, played in the American Negro Leagues, in the Mexican League, and in Cuba. Peter C. Bjarkman, author of *Baseball with a Latin Beat* (McFarland and Co., Inc., 1994) sums up Dihigo's great baseball career this way: "He played a rich diamond music that fell upon the deaf ears of a white-oriented sports press. His concert halls always lay far off the beaten baseball paths."

A terrific pitcher, in 1937 Dihigo threw the first no-hitter recorded in the Mexican League. He threw no-hitters in three different countries: Mexico, Puerto Rico, and Venezuela. In 1938 he posted eighteen wins and two losses in the Mexican League, with an ERA of 0.90.

That same year, Dihigo won the batting crown with a .387 average. "El Maestro," as fans nicknamed him, hit only .179 when he started out. The curve ball baffled him. But Dihigo practiced and practiced, and within two years he was smashing the curve ball, batting .301. In the United States, playing for Negro Leagues teams, he batted .421 in 1926.

In addition to being a great pitcher and a great hitter, Dihigo was also a phenomenal second baseman. Standing 6'4" tall, he had tremendous range and could reach out and stop the ball in any direction.

At one time, many major leaguers went to the Caribbean to play during the winter. Johnny Mize, first baseman for the St. Louis Cardinals, himself a Hall of Famer, played there. "The greatest player I ever saw was a black man," said Mize. "His name is Martin Dihigo. I played with him in Santo Domingo in winter ball in 1943. . . . He was the only guy I ever saw who could play all nine positions, run and was a switch hitter. I thought I was havin' a pretty good year myself down there and they were walkin' him to get to me."

Buck Leonard, also a Hall of Fame member, played in the Negro Leagues with Dihigo. "He was the greatest all-around player I know," said Leonard. "I'd say he was the best ballplayer of all time, black or white. . . . If he's not the greatest, I don't know who is. You take your Ruths, Cobbs, and DiMaggios. Give me Dihigo."

From *Reading Baseball*, published by Good Year Books. Copyright © 1997 Barbara Gregorich and Christopher Jennison.

ACTIVITIES

A *cause* comes first, its *effect* later. An earthquake (cause) shakes the ground and highways buckle (effect). Read each sentence below and fill in its cause or effect.

1. **Cause:** Martin Dihigo practices hitting the curve ball.

   Effect: _____

2. **Cause:** Dihigo is a phenomenal player in three different countries.

   Effect: _____

3. **Cause:** He is a black man, an African Cuban with dark skin.

   Effect: _____

4. **Cause:** _____
   Effect: Pitchers actually prefer to throw to hard-hitting Johnny Mize.

5. **Cause:** _____
   Effect: He is an excellent second baseman.

6. **Cause:** _____
   Effect: Sports reporters do not write about Martin Dihigo.

7. **Cause:** _____
   Effect: He is nicknamed "El Maestro," or "The Master."

From *Reading Baseball*, published by Good Year Books. Copyright © 1997 Barbara Gregorich and Christopher Jennison.

How to Be a Person First

I was ten years old in 1950 when I discovered that my town, Rockford, Illinois, was home not only to me but to the Rockford Peaches, a team of girls and women, who were playing professional baseball. Not softball, but baseball.

The Peaches were one of the best teams in the All-American Girls Baseball League. The owners wanted the women to "look like girls and play like men." The girls played in skirts, but they played so well that everyone came to the ballpark to see their hitting and double plays, not their legs, which were always scraped up from sliding into base anyway.

Mom and Dad took me to as many games as possible. I cheered for the Peaches and was thrilled when they won, sad when they lost. I went to fan picnics and collected their autographs on handsome black-and-white photos. I cut out newspaper articles and pasted them in a scrapbook. After the 1954 season, I was devastated when the League went out of existence. The whole country got the idea that women weren't supposed to play baseball or work in offices or factories anymore, but were supposed to stay home and cook and have babies. It was a very sad time.

The Peaches were so important to me, though, that I kept all my scrapbooks and pictures in boxes that I carried around with me everywhere. When I was fifty years old, I decided to find the women who had been my heroes and ask them about their lives and what it had meant to them to play professional baseball.

I especially remember one of my favorites, Dorothy "Snookie" Doyle, who had played shortstop for the Peaches. She told me how hard it was to keep playing baseball as a little girl when everyone except her mother wanted her to stop. She told me:

My teacher wanted to stop me, but I'd go home and still be playin' ball with the boys. We would play "burnout." They'd try to throw at me as hard as I could take it. Their mother would get upset with me because she thought they were being too hard on me, but I loved it!

My mother had gotten me a catcher's mitt by that time and a baseball uniform when I was only five. My mother was a great baseball fan. She didn't bring me up to be a boy, though, she brought me up to be a person.

What I learned from the Rockford Peaches is that what matters is not whether you're a boy or a girl. You can do anything you want to do if you enjoy it and are good enough at it. Like Snookie says, remember, you're a person first.

—Susan Johnson

By permission of Susan E. Johnson, author of *When Women Played Hardball* (Seattle: Seal Press, 1994).

From *Reading Baseball*, published by Good Year Books. Copyright © 1997 Barbara Gregorich and Christopher Jennison.

Activities

1. List four things that Susan did when she was ten years old.

   a) _____

   b) _____

   c) _____

   d) _____

2. List three things that Susan did when she was fifty years old.

   a) _____

   b) _____

   c) _____

3. Susan Johnson doesn't tell you in this article, but she did something with all the interviews she had with the AAGBL ballplayers. Can you figure out what she did?

   _____

   _____

4. How was Snookie Doyle's life different from that of most girls because her mother bought her a baseball uniform when she was five years old and a catcher's mitt later?

   _____

   _____

   _____

5. How was Susan Johnson's life influenced by seeing women play excellent baseball?

   _____

   _____

   _____

6. Write another title for this story.

   _____

   _____

HUMONGOUS TRIVIA

"So," says Mac as we walk past the baseball field, "ready for a little trivia?"

I groan. Then, just in case he missed it, I make a gagging sound. Mac is my best friend, but he's way into this baseball trivia stuff, which drives me wacko. Mac's name is Kieran McIlhenny, but we call each other by our last names, sort of, 'cause that's cool. I don't mind a bit of trivia now and then, but the problem with Mac is, the trivia questions he asks are really little trivia. I mean, dinky trivia. Things nobody but a nerd could possibly know. Mac doesn't look like a nerd, but sometimes I wonder. Besides, I'd rather be out on the field practicing.

"Sure you are," says Mac, ignoring my sounds. "Gene DeMontreville and Lee DeMontreville."

See what I mean? He drops two names on me and expects me to tell him who they are and what record they hold. I never heard of these guys in my life. "Father and son," I guess, "both pitched shutouts on the same day in history."

"Not even close. They weren't pitchers. And they weren't father and son. Here's another clue. Al Hollingsworth and Bonnie Hollingsworth."

"Bonnie?" I ask. "There was a woman in the major leagues?"

"Get with it, Chris. 'Bonnie' was his nickname. It means awesome." Mac kicks a stone and watches it bounce across the street.

How can I get with it when I never heard of these guys either? I clue him in and he tells me that Al Hollingsworth pitched in the majors for eleven years. So now he's into pitchers. "Four players, at least one of them a pitcher," I say. "What could they have in common?"

"They hold a major league record," he tells me. "Fewer than twenty players hold this record."

I groan again. I don't mind when Mac asks me big trivia, like what was Ty Cobb's batting average, or how many home runs did Hank Aaron clobber. It's the little bitty trivia that drives me wacko. We walk by the swimming pool, and I wonder if maybe I should just push Mac in.

"Austin Knickerbocker and Bill Knickerbocker," he says, coming to a stop.

"They're all brothers, or cousins, maybe, and they all played exactly eleven years," I guess.

Mac rolls his eyes. "Lou Schiappacasse and Ossee Schreckengost."

"Oh, right. That's the clue," I say, "Ossee Schreckengost. Everybody's heard of good old Ossee. He plays first base for the New York Yankees, right?"

Continued on page 48

From *Reading Baseball*, published by Good Year Books. Copyright © 1997 Barbara Gregorich and Christopher Jennison.

HUMONGOUS TRIVIA

"He played a hundred years ago," says Mac.

We start walking again, around and around the pool, and I think if I nudge Mac and he falls in, I can say it was an accident. "Okay, I got it. These are guys nobody ever heard of. That's the record they hold, right?"

"Wrong. Kirk Dressendorfer, Ken Raffensberger, Steve Wojciechowski, and Bill VanLandingham. Give up?"

"Yeah. Just get it over with. Tell me what big thing these guys with the impossible names have in common."

Mac stares at me. "I think maybe you're on the verge of getting it, Chris. Want to keep on trying?"

"No way."

"Okay. They belong to the very select group of major leaguers with the biggest last names—thirteen letters."

I put my hands on Mac's shoulders, like I'm about to say something important, but what I really have in mind is pushing him into the deep end. I'm just about to do it, too, when something zaps through my brain. "Wait a minute," I say. "You mean no major leaguer has ever had a last name longer than thirteen letters?"

"That's right."

"Wow!" I leave Mac standing there as I run toward the baseball diamond.

"Hey, Christopherson! Where you going?" he shouts after me.

"To practice!"

From *Reading Baseball*, published by Good Year Books. Copyright © 1997 Barbara Gregorich and Christopher Jennison.

Activities

Study the definitions below. Each goes with one of the words used in the story. Write the letter of the correct word next to each definition.

_____ 1. extremely large, enormous   **a.** wacko
_____ 2. unimportant matters, inessential things   **b.** zap
_____ 3. small   **c.** awesome
_____ 4. to hit suddenly and forcefully   **d.** humongous
_____ 5. socially correct, popular, outstanding   **f.** trivia
_____ 6. crazy   **g.** nerd
_____ 7. a person who is brilliant but a social misfit   **h.** dinky
_____ 8. outstanding, excellent   **i.** cool

Draw a conclusion about the story and situation to answer each of the questions below.

1. Which of the two friends is more athletic? _____

2. Where does Mac most likely get all his baseball knowledge?

_____

3. What conclusion can you draw about the average length of last names in America?

_____

_____

4. What conclusions can you draw about Chris's personality?

_____

_____

5. If Chris ever makes the major leagues, he will set a new record. Which one?

_____

_____

From *Reading Baseball*, published by Good Year Books. Copyright © 1997 Barbara Gregorich and Christopher Jennison.

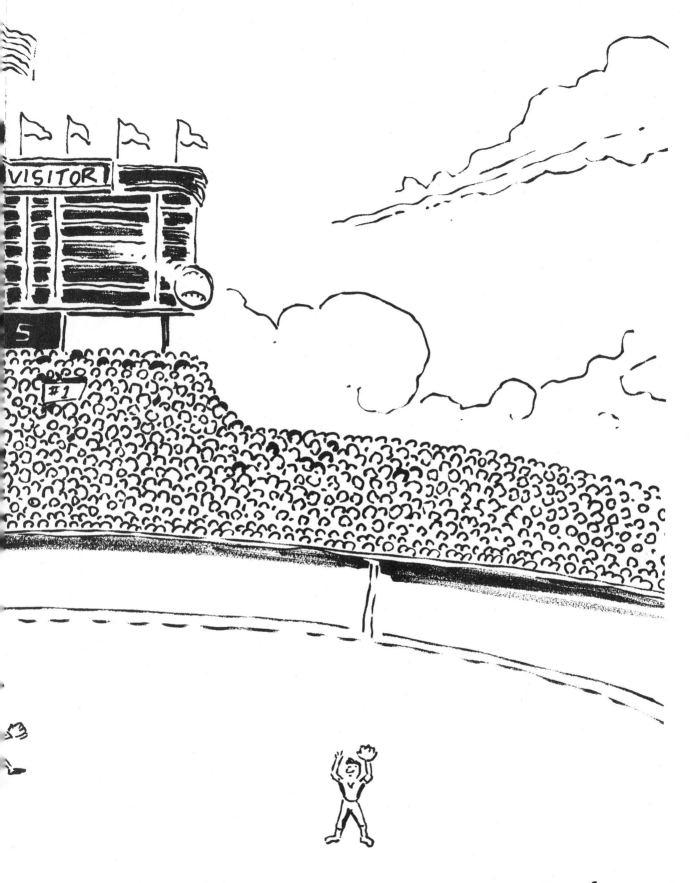

PROJECTS

Best Dressed

Until the early 1970s, when light knit fabrics were introduced, baseball uniforms were made mostly of wool flannel. Imagine playing baseball on a hot and humid day, wearing a long-sleeved wool uniform, a heavy undershirt, and long, woolen stockings. It was not unusual for players to lose five to ten pounds during a game played on a 100-degree day.

The first baseball uniforms were plain and formal looking, but by the beginning of the 1900s teams added colored trim, stripes, and embroidered lettering to brighten up their outfits. In 1916 the New York Giants' uniforms featured thin lines of purple that crisscrossed, creating a plaid effect. Other teams added birds, elephants, and bear cubs to their shirt fronts, and in 1921 the Cleveland Indians wore "World Champions" across their jerseys to celebrate their World Series victory of 1920.

In 1976 the Chicago White Sox adopted an even more unusual uniform that included a navy blue jersey worn outside the belt, like a pajama top. For some games the players wore Bermuda-length shorts. Not only were the shorts impractical, but the players disliked wearing them. The 1944 Brooklyn Dodgers sported strange uniforms too. Night games were a novelty then, and the Dodgers wore uniforms made of a satin material that shone brightly in the artificial light. For night games on the road the Dodgers donned powder-blue satin uniforms. Prior to that time, teams almost always wore gray uniforms when they were traveling.

Numbers on uniforms didn't appear until 1916, when the Indians affixed small numerals to their left sleeves. The New York Yankees first wore numbers on the backs of their jerseys in 1929. At that time, a player's uniform number designated his position in the batting order. Babe Ruth usually hit third, so he was given number 3, which he wore for the rest of his career. In 1960 the White Sox became the first team to display players' names on the backs of their jerseys. Today all teams in the majors include player names on their uniforms except the Yankees.

Maybe the early players weren't so tough after all. In those days loose and baggy uniforms were easy to hit unintentionally with a pitch, giving the batter a free trip to first. Today's close-fitting uniforms mean that the ball must smack a hitter on some part of his body before he gets a free trip to first.

PROJECTS

1. What is the effect of climate or playing conditions on baseball uniforms? Think about this, then make a chart that explains what the ideal uniform for each of the following conditions would be: (a) outdoors in the North during April, September, and October; (b) outdoors in the South during June, July, and August; (c) in domed stadiums anywhere.

2. At the library, read a book or magazine articles about the All-American Girls Baseball League that played from 1943–1954. Write a report describing what the AAGBL uniforms looked like and explain why the players had to wear such uniforms.

3. Imagine that you are a ballplayer in the year 1880. You wear a heavy flannel uniform, you have only one such uniform, and you are responsible for keeping it clean so that you look professional when you step out onto the field. Write a diary covering a week's worth of playing baseball. Describe what happened to your uniform each day, what you did about it, and how you felt about it.

4. Design a baseball uniform for the year 2050. Create sketches and write a description of the sketches. Pay attention to team colors, logo, and the difference between home uniforms and road uniforms.

5. Look at the uniforms on the inside covers of this book. Choose three of the uniforms and write a short fashion report on them imagining that you are a "gentlemen's fashions" reporter of that time. Inform the public what they look like, what you think of them, and whether you think the style will be short-lived or will be around for a long time.

Two Haiku

A haiku is a Japanese verse form of three unrhymed lines. The first and third lines contain five syllables, the middle line contains seven.

Angle

High foul behind third
Left in and out fields converge
Shortstop makes the play.

—Mark Schraf

Roberto

When they called you "Bob"
You felt they were trying to
Steal your heritage.

From *Reading Baseball*, published by Good Year Books. Copyright © 1997 Barbara Gregorich and Christopher Jennison.

Used by permission of Mark Schraf, who is a free-lance baseball author and fiction editor of *Spitball: The Literary Baseball Magazine.*

PROJECTS

1. Write your own haiku about baseball—the game, the players, the fans, how you feel, anything.

2. Draw a diagram of a baseball field. Write the numbers from 1–9 in each of the positions, starting with 1 for the pitcher, 2 for the catcher, 3 for the first baseman, and so on. (If you don't know the correct numbering, look it up in a score book or in the library or ask somebody.) Using a ruler and a different colored pencil or ink than the one you used on the diagram, draw what happens in the haiku entitled "Angle." Make certain you draw an angle to show what happens in the poem.

3. A paraphrase is a restatement of something in a simpler way. Write a brief paraphrase of "Angle."

4. A monologue is a dramatic speech by one person, usually in a play. Write a monologue from Roberto Clemente's point of view, telling what he feels when the players call him "Bob."

5. Read about the culture of Puerto Rico, where Roberto Clemente was born. Write a brief report on the customs of the people: what foods they eat, which holidays they celebrate, which leisure-time activities they consider important, how they express friendship.

The Spark That Lit the Fire

In 1988 Kirk Gibson, formerly a Tiger, played 150 games for the Los Angeles Dodgers, hitting twenty-five home runs. His slugging helped the Dodgers win the division title, but 1988 was a bad year for Gibson. Because of numerous leg injuries, by season's end he could only limp around the base paths.

In the National League Championship Series, the Dodgers faced the New York Mets. The Mets had trounced the Boys in Blue ten out of eleven games that season. But thanks to the pitching of Orel Hershiser and Tim Belcher, and to the hitting of Mike Scioscia and Gibson, the Dodgers won the NLCS in seven games. In that series Gibson hit a home run in the twelfth inning of the fourth game to give the Dodgers a 5–4 victory, then homered in the fifth game to help them win, 7–4.

Meanwhile, the Oakland A's took only four games to win the American League Championship Series. The A's were loaded with power: Jose Canseco, Dave Henderson, Mark McGwire, Dave Parker, and Tony Phillips. Dave Stewart was their unstoppable pitcher and Dennis Eckersley their unsinkable reliever. Managed by Tony LaRussa, whom many consider the best manager in baseball today, the A's were expected to wallop the injury-ridden, not-very-powerful Dodgers.

The first encounter took place in Los Angeles. Kirk Gibson's leg injuries were so debilitating that he sat in the training room, not in the dugout. Nobody expected him to play. By the bottom of the sixth, the A's were winning, 4–3. When the top of the ninth ended, the score stood at 4–3. Dennis Eckersley took the mound for Oakland. He got two outs on the Dodgers, then walked a batter. Even with the tying run on base, all Eckersley had to do was retire pitcher Alejandro Pena—or whomever the Dodgers sent in to pinch hit for Pena—and the A's would win the first game . . . and, as everybody believed, the World Series.

Gibson had a feeling he would be called upon to bat, so he limped into the tunnel leading to the dugout and began loosening up, swinging his bat against a padded column. *Ka-thunk! Ka-thunk!* The sound reverberated through the concrete and shook the dugout.

Dodger manager Tommy LaSorda called upon him to pinch-hit for Pena. A gallant but sorry sight, Gibson stood at the plate to face baseball's greatest relief pitcher. In Dodger Stadium, 56,000 fans rose to their feet and stood for his entire at-bat.

Kirk Gibson fouled off two pitches, then worked the count to 3–2. The Eck was one strike away from an Oakland victory. But any pitch can be turned around, and Gibson turned around the next one—blasting a home run, giving the Dodgers a 5–4 win, and creating pandemonium among the fans at the ballpark and the millions watching on television. The news footage of Gibson limping around the base paths is shown again and again as one of the great moments in baseball.

Kirk Gibson did not appear in any of the other World Series games that year. But his only at-bat was the spark that lit the fire, inspiring the Dodgers to roar over the dazed Oakland team and win the World Series four games to one.

From *Reading Baseball*, published by Good Year Books. Copyright © 1997 Barbara Gregorich and Christopher Jennison.

PRojecTs

1. Read the poem "Casey at the Bat" (page 70 of this book). Using the same rhythm and rhyme scheme as "Casey," write a poem about Gibson at the bat.

2. View a video that shows the first game of the 1988 World Series, or a video that shows highlights of that Series. As you watch Gibson's at-bat, act as the radio announcer, describing it as it happens for the fans listening on radio.

3. At the library, find accounts of Kirk Gibson's leg injuries during the 1988 season. Draw a diagram of the human leg (left and right), showing bones, muscles, and nerves. Use arrows, circles, and short descriptions to show Gibson's injuries.

4. Imagine that Kirk Gibson and Dennis Eckersley are sitting next to each other as spectators at a future World Series. Write about their encounter as if it were a scene in a play.

5. What percentage of major league baseball games do you think are won in the last inning? Write your guess on a sheet of paper. Next to it, write your guess on the percentage of major league games won in the very last at-bat. Use a library or a computer online source to find information on the subject. Write the correct percentage next to each of your guesses. How close or how far off were your guesses?

You Can't Play in Skirts

The second of three daughters, Alta was born to George and Lucinda Weiss on February 9, 1890, in Ragersville, Ohio. Legend has it that Alta could hurl a corncob at the family cat with all the wrist-snap and follow-through of a major leaguer—at the tender age of two.

As a child, Alta loved the outdoors and hated housework of all sorts. Encouraged by her father, she became an excellent shot with rifle and shotgun and enjoyed hunting. In college she played basketball and tennis. But Alta was also a pianist, a singer, and a violinist who played with a dance band and, in the beginning, she played baseball in a skirt. Of all her skills and talents, baseball remained her true interest in life.

It's highly unlikely, however, that either George Weiss or his daughter had in mind that she would become a semipro ballplayer. That happened quite by accident, when the family was vacationing in Vermilion, Ohio, in the summer of 1907. There, Alta approached a group of young men and asked to play catch with them. Perhaps they were amused, perhaps chivalrous. But when their gloves stopped smoking and their hands stopped stinging, they were in awe.

Seeing the young vacationer play, Mayor H. P. Williams suggested to the manager of the semipro Vermilion Independents that he sign the seventeen-year-old, long-haired player who wore a skirt. When Charles Heidloff refused, Williams arranged for a game between two local teams, with Alta pitching for one of them. Striking out fifteen men in that game, Alta set the large crowd buzzing. In a second game, she fanned nine batters. Heidloff changed his mind and asked her to join his team.

On September 2, 1907, Alta, wearing a long blue skirt, took the mound in Vermilion in her first semi-pro game. Hurling five innings, she gave up four hits and one run. For the remainder of the eleven-inning game, she played first base. The Vermilion Independents won, 4–3.

Although a reporter strongly advised her to wear pants, she would never have listened to such advice. But she did listen to baseball, and the game taught her the folly of clinging to this particular notion of femininity. "I found that you can't play ball in skirts," she explained. "I tried. I wore a skirt over my bloomers—and nearly broke my neck. Finally I was forced to discard it, and now I always wear bloomers—but made so wide that the fullness gives a skirtlike effect."

—Barbara Gregorich

From an article originally published in *Timeline,* a publication of the Ohio Historical Society.

From *Reading Baseball,* published by Good Year Books. Copyright © 1997 Barbara Gregorich and Christopher Jennison.

PROjecTs

1. Imagine that you are a newspaper reporter interviewing Alta Weiss. Write a list of ten questions you would ask her.

2. Draw a map of Ohio. Locate Ragersville, Vermilion, and Cleveland on the map. Write a brief information piece on each town, giving its population, founding date (if possible), and any other interesting facts.

3. Certain words in the English language come from people's names. *Sandwich,* for example, refers to the fourth Earl of Sandwich, who ate meat between two slices of bread. Research the word *bloomers* and write a report on the person after whom they are named. In the report, describe what bloomers were, who invented them, and why they were invented.

4. Today women play baseball on the Silver Bullets. If you don't know who the Silver Bullets are or what their uniforms look like, go to the library and find a picture of them in a magazine or newspaper. Then write a "time travel" letter to Alta Weiss, telling her what female baseball players wear today.

5. Alta Weiss attended college and became a medical doctor. Not long after she started to practice, an influenza epidemic ravaged the country. She called this "one of the most distressing periods of my life." Read about the influenza epidemic. Write a report telling when it occurred, what the results were, and why so many people died.

A Day At The Ballpark

This is my first time at Whales Stadium. I find my seat easily. Behind home plate, three rows back. I settle in, balancing two bratwursts and a soft drink on my knee. I study the players out on the field doing their pregame stretches. I listen to the crowd noises around me. *Hot dogs here! Hot dogs! Ice-cold cola!*

The announcer gives the lineup and I fill out my scorecard. The Dragons are in first place by four games. The Whales are in second. The Dragons go down one-two-three and the Whales come to bat. The Dragons' pitcher winds up and throws. A ball. *Good eye! Good eye!* The next pitch is a called strike. *Hey, blue, can't you see?!* The third pitch comes in, and Deegan sends it through the hole at second base. *Keep it up, keep it up, everybody hit!* Husnick steps to the plate.

By the top of the fourth the Dragons are winning, 4–1. Our pitcher throws to Bratz, their best hitter. Ball. *What was wrong with that one, ump?* We keep the Dragons from scoring more runs. Our shortstop comes to bat. *Deegan! Take it downtown, baby.* Deegan is caught looking and I record it on my scorecard. *Deegan, you're a bum!* Husnick fouls a ball over the screen. I turn to stare as it goes over the roof and into the parking lot. *Crash!* The sound of glass breaking comes over the loudspeaker. Everybody laughs. Husnick fouls the next pitch. *Atta boy, Tony, you got a piece of it.* Husnick hits a double, and the Whales have a runner in scoring position. The pitch comes in and the ump calls it a strike. *Now you've seen it, Davis. Hey, blue, where's your glasses?* Davis steps out of the batter's box and knocks dirt off his cleats. *Take him to the bridge, baby.* Davis connects and the ball rises as it races toward the fence. We're all on our feet. Yes! It's a home run. We've cut the Dragons' lead to one run now. *C'mon, fish, let's spout off!*

Top of the seventh, score still 4–3. *Attention, attention! Brats are now on sale, two for one.* The Whales send in a new pitcher. I mark his name and number on my scorecard. *Hear that? Brats are two for one. When they get down to three for one, I'll buy some.* The Dragons' batter goes down swinging at the next three pitches. The next batter is Bratz. *Hey, look! Two-for-one is up!* The ump calls a ball. *Y'er blind!* Bratz singles to left. The next batter hits into a double play and it's time for the seventh-inning stretch. We all stand and sing "Take Me Out to the Ballgame." The Whales come to bat. *Get some wood on it, baby! Take it for a ride!* We tie the score, 4–4.

It stays that way until the bottom of the ninth, when Davis hits a solo home run. We all jump to our feet and cheer. Davis runs around the bases and slaps the hands of his teammates. I fill in my scorecard. On my way out, I buy tickets to next week's game.

From *Reading Baseball*, published by Good Year Books. Copyright © 1997 Barbara Gregorich and Christopher Jennison.

From *Reading Baseball*, published by Good Year Books. Copyright © 1997 Barbara Gregorich and Christopher Jennison.

NAME _____   DATE _____

PROjecTs

1. Go to a baseball game. Take a notebook with you. Write down all the baseball-related comments that you hear. Exchange your comments with somebody who went to a different baseball game. Which were your favorite comments? Do you think baseball slang is more interesting than other sports slang? Why or why not?

2. Believe it or not, there was once a major league team called the Whales. Do some detective work to discover who the Whales were, in which league they played, where and when they played, and the names of the teams they played against.

3. Make a chart showing a typical ballpark meal. Next to each food item, give its nutritional content. List protein, carbohydrate, and fat grams. Also list calories. At the bottom of the chart, write a nutritional analysis of this meal.

4. What kind of person do you think the narrator of this story is? Read the story a few times, looking for clues. Then write a paragraph or two about the narrator.

5. Minor league teams sponsor many different kinds of promotions to get fans to attend their games. Some teams select one or two fans a game to race against somebody on the team for a cash prize; other teams draw names and give away small or large prizes. Imagine that you have been hired as promotions director for the Whales. What would you do to get more fans to come to the ballpark? Write down ten different ideas for increasing attendance.

Fantasy Baseball

Fantasy baseball is a game based on major league statistics of ballplayers. Twelve people form a fantasy league based on either American or National League players. Each of the twelve becomes an "owner" with 260 unit credits. A unit is usually worth a dollar, although it can be worth fifty cents or twenty cents or whatever the owners decide. At the beginning of each season, the owners form teams at a draft, where they bid real money on real ballplayers. This money is kept in a "pot." No owner can spend more than 260 credits on his or her team. Owners then keep track of the batting and pitching statistics of their players. They win or lose points depending on how their batters do in four specific batting statistics. They also win or lose points for their pitchers in four pitching statistics. At the end of the season, the owner with the highest number of points wins. Usually the prize is at least half of the money in the pot.

Letters to the Editor

I'm twelve years old and I've been playing fantasy baseball for three years. I think it's cool that I can play in a league with my dad and his friends. Last year I won! My sister, who's only eight, is going to play next year. Boys and girls can play in the same league as adults. Or kids can form their own leagues. You don't even have to live in the same place to be in the same league. You can even form a league on the Internet.

Ty Zeckman

Get real. Baseball is a game played outdoors, in the sun and rain. It takes physical skill to play ball. Fantasy is all in the head. If a fantasy team wins, that doesn't mean the same team would win in real life. Real wins depend on runs scored, not on all those other numbers. It's feet running across home plate that count, not numbers added on paper.

Pat Ingstrup

By playing fantasy baseball, owners can see their judgment validated or invalidated. They can learn to make sound decisions based on facts, not on emotions. I don't mind that my son and daughter play fantasy baseball, because they both play in Little League, also. As long as they play both physical and intellectual games, I'm happy.

A father

"Fantasy" is the perfect name for it, all right. It's the "baseball" that's wrong. Fantasy baseball really has nothing to do with baseball. It's a game of numbers, and the numbers could be from any sport: football, basketball, you name it. They could even be numbers from the financial pages. Count me out.

A real baseball fan

PRojecTs

1. Write your own "Letter to the Editor" on the subject of fantasy baseball. Make certain the letter is no more than 100 words long and that it states your opinion clearly.

2. Read about the rules of fantasy baseball in a book, newspaper, or magazine. Make a chart showing how an owner gets points. Use real-life players to show how the point system works.

3. Write a science fiction story that goes beyond fantasy baseball. Imagine baseball teams composed of robots. Write a story in which something happens either to a robot player, to a team, to a fan, or to somebody else connected with baseball. Make the story as exciting and thought-provoking as you can.

4. Many fantasy baseball leagues reserve 10 percent of the pot money for the owner who comes up with the best name for his or her fantasy team. Often the winning names are word plays, such as puns on the owner's last name or jokes about the owner's dreams. Make up a fantasy league of twelve teams. Name the league and name each of the twelve teams.

5. Use a computer to browse the Internet and World Wide Web pages for fantasy baseball information. Download some of the information and print it out. Write a report on what you find.

The Detroit Tigers

A capital *D* in an Old English script emblazons their hats and uniforms. They are the Detroit Tigers, one of the oldest clubs in the major leagues. Since their formation in 1901, the Tigers have experienced three waves of greatness. Although the new team got off to a bad start its first few years, the first wave of greatness came very soon—in 1907, when a young right fielder named Ty Cobb joined the team. In his first full season, Cobb led the American League in batting average, hits, RBIs, and stolen bases.

Outfielders Sam Crawford and Harry Heilmann played on the team with Cobb under manager Hughie Jennings. Cobb, Crawford, Heilmann, and Jennings were all later elected to the Hall of Fame. In 1907, their sixth year of existence, the Tigers won the pennant but lost the World Series to the Chicago Cubs. In 1908 Detroit again won the pennant but lost the Series to the Cubs. For a third straight year, Detroit won the pennant in 1909. This time they lost the Series to the Pittsburgh Pirates.

After the team of 1909, the Tigers declined for a long period. But teams build histories whether or not they win. In one interesting event in Tiger history, Ty Cobb ran into the stands in 1912 in New York and punched a fan who had been heckling him. The president of the American League suspended Cobb, but his teammates went out on strike until his reinstatement.

The second wave of Tiger greatness came in the 1930s, with players such as catcher Mickey Cochrane, first baseman Hank Greenberg, second baseman Charlie Gehringer, and outfielder Goose Goslin. All four are in the Hall of Fame. In 1934 Detroit won the pennant with a 101–53 record. But they lost the World Series to the "Gashouse Gang" St. Louis Cardinals in seven games. Angry that Cardinal Ducky Medwick slid hard into the Tiger third baseman, fans waited until the bottom of the sixth, when Medwick took his position at third base. Then they threw apples, oranges, scorecards, food wrappers, and other litter at Medwick. Baseball

Continued on page 64

From *Reading Baseball*, published by Good Year Books. Copyright © 1997 Barbara Gregorich and Christopher Jennison.

THE DETROIT TIGERS

Commissioner Landis, in attendance that day, ordered Medwick out of the game for his own safety.

Finally, in 1935, the Tigers' time had come. First they won the pennant. Then, led by the hard-hitting G-men (Gehringer, Goslin, Greenberg), they defeated the Chicago Cubs in six games to win their first World Series. In 1940 they won the pennant but lost the Series to Cincinnati; in 1945 they again defeated the Chicago Cubs in the World Series. After that, the Tigers fell to the basement, losing 104 games in 1952.

The third wave of greatness began to build in the early 1960s, thanks to players such as Norm Cash and Rocky Colavito. In 1968 Tiger Denny McLain led the majors with thirty-one wins—the last major league pitcher to have a thirty-win season. McLain and Mickey Lolich pitched the Tigers to the pennant that year and to a World Series victory over the Cardinals. The third wave of greatness receded by 1974, when the Tigers again finished at the bottom.

With players such as Alan Trammell and Lou Whitaker, Detroit won the American League East division title in 1984. The Tigers went on to win the pennant by defeating Kansas City in the League Championship Series. Propelled by the pitching of Jack Morris and Willie Hernandez, as well as by the slugging of Kirk Gibson and Lance Parish, Detroit won the World Series by defeating the San Diego Padres in five games. Despite that wonderful year, no fourth wave of greatness developed for the Tigers. Gibson left the team, as did Parrish, as did Morris.

As the Tigers approach their second century of baseball, they hope to ride the crest of another wave of greatness.

From *Reading Baseball*, published by Good Year Books. Copyright © 1997 Barbara Gregorich and Christopher Jennison.

PROJECTS

1. Research the history of what is today called Tiger Stadium. Give a speech on the history of Tiger Stadium, using photographs, slides, or drawings to illustrate the speech.

2. Certain Midwest cities, such as Detroit, have suffered economic hard times as other cities in different parts of the country have grown. Sometimes baseball owners take their teams out of these older cities and into new cities. With one other person, hold a pro-con debate in front of the class. One of you should take the side of the owner who wants to leave, while the other should take the side of the fans who want the team to stay.

3. Choose one of the Hall-of-Fame Tiger players from the article. Read all you can about this player, and then write the lyrics to a song about him.

4. What is your favorite baseball team? Write a brief team history about it.

5. Write a movie or TV script for the famous incident in which Ty Cobb ran into the stands to punch a heckler.

From *Reading Baseball*, published by Good Year Books. Copyright © 1997 Barbara Gregorich and Christopher Jennison.

Careers in Baseball

You can have a career in baseball in many different ways. You could work for one of the two major leagues; one of the twenty-eight professional teams or their minor league teams; a major newspaper or television station; or a baseball-dependent business.

By far the largest employers are the individual teams, who hire on-field personnel, office personnel, and stadium personnel. You can pursue an on-field career as a ballplayer, of course, if you're talented enough. If you major in sports medicine, you might end up as a trainer.

Baseball clubs employ personnel in management, finance, human resources, publicity, marketing, sales, data, and media and communications.

Many people in the front office of baseball clubs today started out as stadium workers. You can do the same, perhaps handing out giveaways. From there you might move up to working at a concessions stand or cleaning the stadium after a game. Stadium workers include vendors, ushers, security personnel, and the grounds crew. There's also an organist who plays at games, a stadium announcer, and an operator.

Both the American and National leagues employ people in numerous categories: finance, records keeping, publicity, scheduling, and other broad areas. The AL and NL also employ all the major and minor league umpires.

The media hire a large number of people who want careers in baseball. Newspaper reporters and television broadcasters also work other sports during the off-season. Broadcasters employed by individual teams usually work exclusively in baseball.

Finally, there are baseball-dependent businesses. The Baseball Hall of Fame in Cooperstown, New York, for example, employs librarians, archivists, curators, and public relations personnel. Various statistics services hire people interested in both data and baseball. Publishers of baseball cards engage photographers and writers as well as sales and publicity people.

If you love antiques and collectibles, you might find employment working in a memorabilia shop, selling such items to customers.

Architects and designers can have baseball-related careers: there are jobs in stadium architecture as well as in the design of baseball apparel. If manufacturing is your game, there are bats to produce, as well as gloves, hats, and uniforms. Other manufacturers produce stadium seating, batting cages, and travel equipment. In short, there is no shortage of jobs in baseball.

From *Reading Baseball*, published by Good Year Books. Copyright © 1997 Barbara Gregorich and Christopher Jennison.

PROJECTS

1. What is your idea of the perfect job in baseball? Imagine yourself working at such a job. Write a description of everything you do during one day at work, from the time you get there until the time you leave.

2. Imagine that somebody has illegally entered the stadium in or near your hometown and stolen home plate! You are a television reporter interviewing the head of stadium security. What questions would you ask him or her?

3. Read the article on careers in baseball again. Then make a chart showing the employers and in what categories of jobs they employ people.

4. Using a combination of library research and interviews, write a report on the nature of outfield grass, dirt, drainage, and care. Give scientific explanations for everything.

5. Invent a new job in baseball. Write a newspaper press release about the new job. Give it a name and a job description. Explain to the readers why the new job was created.

Casey at the Bat

The outlook wasn't brilliant for
  the Mudville nine that day;
  The score stood four to two with
but one inning more to play.
And then when Cooney died at first,
  and Barrows did the same,
A sickly silence fell upon the patrons
  of the game.

A straggling few got up to go in deep
  despair. The rest
Clung to that hope which springs
  eternal in the human breast;
They thought if only Casey could but
  get a whack at that—
We'd put up even money now with
  Casey at the bat.

But Flynn preceded Casey,
  as did also Jimmy Blake,
And the former was a lulu and the
  latter was a cake;
So upon the stricken multitude
  grim melancholy sat,
For there seemed but little chance of
  Casey's getting to the bat.

But Flynn let drive a single,
  to the wonderment of all,
And Blake, the much despised,
  tore the cover off the ball;
And when the dust had lifted, and
  the men saw what had occurred,
There was Jimmy safe at second and
  Flynn a-hugging third.

Then from 5,000 throats and more
  there rose a lusty yell;

It rumbled through the valley,
  it rattled in the dell,
It knocked upon the mountain and
  recoiled upon the flat,
For Casey, mighty Casey,
  was advancing to the bat.

There was ease in Casey's manner as
  he stepped into his place;
There was pride in Casey's bearing
  and a smile on Casey's face.
And when, responding to the cheers,
  he lightly doffed his hat,
No stranger in the crowd could doubt
  'twas Casey at the bat.

Ten thousand eyes were on him
  as he rubbed his hands with dirt;
Five thousand tongues applauded
  when he wiped them on his shirt.
Then while the writhing pitcher
  ground the ball into his hip,
Defiance gleamed in Casey's eye,
  a sneer curled Casey's lip.

And now the leather-covered sphere
  came hurtling through the air,
And Casey stood a-watching it in
  haughty grandeur there.
Close by the sturdy batsman the ball
  unheeded sped —
"That ain't my style," said Casey.
  "Strike one," the umpire said.

From the bleachers, black with people,
  there went up a muffled roar,

Continued on page 70

From *Reading Baseball*, published by Good Year Books. Copyright © 1997 Barbara Gregorich and Christopher Jennison.

Casey At the Bat

Like the beating of the storm-waves
    on a stern and distant shore.
"Kill him! Kill the umpire!" shouted
    some one on the stand;
And it's likely they'd have killed him
    had not Casey raised his hand.

With a smile of Christian charity
    great Casey's visage shone
He stilled the rising tumult; he bade
    the game go on;
He signaled to the pitcher, and once
    more the spheroid flew;
But Casey still ignored it, and the
    umpire said, "Strike two."

"Fraud!" cried the maddened thou
    sands, and echo answered fraud;
But one scornful look from Casey and
    the audience was awed.
They saw his face grow stern and
    cold, they saw his muscles strain,

And they knew that Casey wouldn't
    let that ball go by again.
The sneer is gone from Casey's lip,
    his teeth are clenched in hate;
He pounds with cruel violence his bat
    upon the plate.
And now the pitcher holds the ball,
    and now he lets it go,
And now the air is shattered by the
    force of Casey's blow.

Oh, somewhere in this favored land
    the sun is shining bright;
The band is playing somewhere,
    and somewhere hearts are light,
And somewhere men are laughing,
    and somewhere children shout;
But there is no joy in Mudville—
    mighty Casey has struck out.

—Ernest Lawrence Thayer
San Francisco Examiner, June 3, 1888

From *Reading Baseball*, published by Good Year Books. Copyright © 1997 Barbara Gregorich and Christopher Jennison.

pRojecTs

1. Draw a detailed map of the imaginary town of Mudville. Label the streets and public buildings. Select ten famous sites in Mudville and number them. Write a brief description for each of the ten sites, telling its importance in Mudville history.

2. Imagine that you were the umpire at this game. That evening, you go back to your hotel room and write a letter to a friend. Write the letter.

3. A magnificent statue stands in the lobby of the National Baseball Hall of Fame Library in Cooperstown, New York. The sculpture, by Mark Lundeen, is of Casey. Is it appropriate that a statue of a fictional hero adorn this lobby? Should it be a statue of Babe Ruth or Ted Williams or Hank Aaron? Write several paragraphs in which you explore the reasons why this statue might stand at the BHOF Library.

4. Many parodies and sequels have been written to "Casey at the Bat," including at least one from the pitcher's point of view and at least one that shows Casey redeeming himself. Find one of these parodies or sequels and read it to the class. Or, write a few paragraphs explaining which of the two poems you liked better and why.

5. Who was Ernest Lawrence Thayer? When did he write "Casey at the Bat"? How did he feel about the fame of his poem? Imagine that you must write a 150-word encyclopedia entry on Ernest Lawrence Thayer, answering these questions. Write the piece so that you give readers the necessary information in an interesting way.

From *Reading Baseball*, published by Good Year Books. Copyright © 1997 Barbara Gregorich and Christopher Jennison.

Earth and Sky

His hands dug the dirt and planted the ivy that climbs the walls of Wrigley Field, and his mind came up with the idea of the exploding scoreboard in Comiskey Park. Bill Veeck infused the game of baseball with life from bottom to top.

William Veeck, Sr., Bill's father, was president of the Chicago Cubs from 1917–1933 and was the first to agree that baseball games should be broadcast over the radio. Bill Veeck, Jr., grew even more innovative than his father—more innovative than any other owner in baseball history. As a young man, he planted the ivy in Wrigley's outfield, but that was just the beginning.

During World War II, Veeck joined the United States Marines and lost a leg in battle. In its place, he wore a wooden leg. Although he was often in pain throughout his life, he joked about it. "I'll bet my feet are only half as cold as yours," he would say on a cold night at the ballpark.

As owner of the minor league Milwaukee Brewers, he agreed that the All-American Girls Baseball League could play in his stadium in 1944. In 1946 he bought his first major league team, the Cleveland Indians, and in 1947 signed the American League's first black player, Larry Doby. The following year, the Indians won the pennant and the World Series, with 2.6 million fans attending games.

By 1951 Veeck owned the lowest-standing team in baseball, the St. Louis Browns (who later became the Baltimore Orioles). To attract fans, he thought up many different stunts. The one for which he will be forever remembered was his hiring of Eddie Gaedel, who stood 3'7" tall, to take one at-bat and draw a walk for the Browns. The opposing pitcher couldn't find Gaedel's tiny strike zone and did walk him.

In 1959 Bill Veeck bought the Chicago White Sox. That year, the team won its first pennant in forty years. Veeck created the exploding scoreboard that became identified with Comiskey Park. When the old park was torn down, a replica scoreboard was built in the new Comiskey. Veeck sold the Sox, then bought them again in 1976. To draw fans, he sponsored giveaways and designed old-fashioned uniforms for the players. Due to ill heath and lack of finances, Veeck sold the Sox in 1981.

Bill Veeck died on January 2, 1986. As Chicagoans and the nation mourned his passing, the trumpeter at his funeral played Aaron Copland's "Fanfare for the Common Man." Bill Veeck knew that baseball has its roots in the soil, its celebrations in the sky, and its life in the heart of the common, everyday fan.

From *Reading Baseball*, published by Good Year Books. Copyright © 1997 Barbara Gregorich and Christopher Jennison.

PROjecTs

1. Bill Veeck was elected to the Baseball Hall of Fame in 1991. Study the wording of BHOF plaques; you can see them on certain baseball cards or reproduced in books. Write a BHOF plaque for Bill Veeck, following the style of the other plaques.

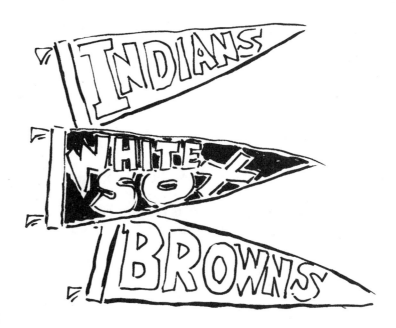

2. Read *Veeck as in Wreck,* Bill Veeck's autobiography (New York: Simon & Schuster, 1989). After reading it, make a world map and label the places where Veeck lived, fought, or worked. Number each spot in chronological order and write a brief "Veeck was here" item for each.

3. Look up the word *maverick* in a dictionary and think about its meaning. Hold a class debate on the topic "Does Society Need Mavericks?"

4. Use the library periodicals section to find information on Mike Veeck, Bill's son. Is Mike Veeck, owner of the St. Paul Saints, like his father or different? Argue your position in a few paragraphs.

5. How would you behave if you owned a major league baseball team? Think about this, then write a list of the ten most important things you, as an owner, would remember in dealing with players, fans, personnel, and other owners. Label the list "I Shall Not" and begin each of the ten behaviors with this phrase.

Sea Dogs and Snappers

At first, baseball players wore caps to protect themselves from the sun and wind and to shade their eyes as they watched the ball leave the bat. Ballplayers still wear caps to protect them from the elements—and because a cap is part of the baseball uniform.

Caps are part of the lucrative baseball business, too. Much of each team's money comes from the sale of merchandise, such as caps, T-shirts, uniform shirts, and jackets all printed with the team's name and logo.

Several years ago, when the Chicago White Sox adopted new black-and-silver uniforms and old-fashioned logos, they sold more merchandise than any other team in baseball. Then along came two new teams, the Colorado Rockies and the Florida Marlins, and soon the Rockies' purple, black, and silver caps sold more than the White Sox caps.

This points out an interesting trend in baseball. For decades most major league teams kept the same name, the same logo, and the same colors. Today teams change logos and colors more often or redesign them for a fresh new look that just might sell more merchandise.

Minor league teams can make even more changes more often. This is because major league teams have longer histories. The Cincinnati Reds have been around since 1875. They are not about to change their name to the "Queen City Greens"—this would be such a drastic break with tradition that it could drive people away.

But minor league teams come and go. One year a minor league team may be owned by the Cleveland Indians, then by the Florida Marlins, then by the Los Angeles Dodgers. Today minor league teams see these changes as a great opportunity. They hire "merchandising consultants" who take surveys of what people like. A consultant will help a team choose its new colors, its new name, and its new logo. The Portland, Oregon, team's nickname is the Sea Dogs, its colors teal and white. The logo is the words *Sea Dogs,* with a large letter *P.* A fierce-looking seal with a bat in its mouth looks through the opening in the letter. The Beloit, Wisconsin, team's nickname is the "Snappers." The logo is a scowling snapper turtle with a bat over its shoulder.

Today baseball caps do more than keep off the rain and block out the sun. They bring in big money for baseball owners—and just maybe they give those who wear them a sense of pride and style.

From *Reading Baseball,* published by Good Year Books. Copyright © 1997 Barbara Gregorich and Christopher Jennison.

PRojecTs

From *Reading Baseball*, published by Good Year Books. Copyright © 1997 Barbara Gregorich and Christopher Jennison.

1. Imagine a player from the early 1900s (Babe Ruth, perhaps) meeting a player from the Florida Marlins, Seattle Mariners, or other expansion team today. Write a scene in which the two players meet and comment on each other's uniforms.

2. Suppose that you have to come up with a name, logo, colors, and uniform for a new baseball team. What questions would you ask people your own age about what they like in colors, logos, and names? Write out at least ten survey questions to ask. Remember that survey questions must be designed to be answered rapidly, with either yes or no or a rating scale of some sort.

3. Do some on-line research about two different minor league teams. Write a report on what you learned about each team solely through online research.

4. Research either the teams of the Negro Leagues or the teams of the All-American Girls Baseball League. Choose three of the teams within either league, and then write a report giving the history of the team names and describing their uniform designs and colors.

5. Imagine that your town is getting a new minor league baseball team next year. The local newspaper holds a contest to name the team. Write a "Letter to the Editor" explaining what name you think the team should have and why.

THIRD-BASE BELLE

Madeline English, called "Maddy" by her friends and fans, joined the All-American Girls Baseball League before she even graduated from high school in Everett, Massachusetts. She headed west to the Wrigley Field tryouts with two other New Englanders, Mary Pratt and Dorothy Green. All three made the cut, with Maddy going to the Racine Belles and Mary and Dottie to the Rockford Peaches. Their teammates soon referred to the New England trio as "Maddy, Pratty, and Dottie."

Because her older brother Edward played third base, Maddy had chosen that position on her Massachusetts softball team. "I emulated him," she says, "copied the way he threw and everything. He'd have liked to kill me for that." Volunteering to play the hot corner for Racine, she was voted to the All-Star teams in 1946 and 1948 for what league managers called her "extremely aggressive play."

In 1948 English set an AAGBL record for chances at third base—an incredible 589. "I went after everything," she explains, "and they counted it all. I also had the most errors that year. If I reached over the fence for the ball, they gave me an error. Once I went over the railing to get a ball and ended up sliding under the bleachers. My uniform was all black when I came back on the field."

Maddy describes life at the hot corner with nonchalance. "When it was hit to you," she says, "it was hit so hard you either got it or you didn't. And if it hit you and fell down, there was still time to pick it up and throw the runner out."

A third baseman must always be ready for a bunt, and this was even more true in the AAGBL, where players bunted well. "Dottie Kamenshek and Marge Callaghan were lefties," English recalls. "They were my nemeses. If they saw me creeping in, they'd lengthen the bat and hit [the ball] right at me. I'd get hit in the shoulder, arm, chest. But you pick up the ball, throw it to first, and then say 'Ouch!'"

From 1943–1950, Maddy English played for the Racine Belles. After the team folded, she went back to playing softball, only to discover that she no longer liked it. "It was less challenging than hardball," she says. So she returned to Everett and attended Boston University, graduating in 1956. She then taught physical education at Everett Junior High School. After earning her Masters degree in 1962 she ended up teaching literature and history and, finally, being a high school guidance counselor.

From *Reading Baseball*, published by Good Year Books. Copyright © 1997 Barbara Gregorich and Christopher Jennison.

PROJECTS

1. Why is third base, and not first base, called the hot corner? Talk to a science teacher or physics teacher about the trajectory and speed of a ground ball hit hard by a right-handed batter to either corner. Look through the index of a few books on the science of sports to see if you can find the answer to this question. Create a chart showing a diagram of the infield. Draw a curved line from home to third to represent a hit ball and draw a similar line from home to first. In the margins of the chart, explain the difference.

2. Max Carey, a member of the Baseball Hall of Fame, said that the greatest baseball game he ever saw was the sixth game of the 1946 Shaughnessy Series between the Rockford Peaches and the Racine Belles. Research this game and create either a line score or a box score to show what happened. Beneath the score, write a seventy-five-words-or-less summary of the game.

3. There are fewer third basemen in the Baseball Hall of Fame than there are players from the other eight positions. Choose one of the third basemen in the BHOF and write a report on him.

4. When Maddy English arrived in Racine, Wisconsin, she found it very different from Everett, Massachusetts. Read about Racine. When was it settled and by whom? What is its ethnic makeup? What kind of industry exists there? What kind of weather does the region have? Draw a map of Wisconsin showing the location of Racine. Write a history of the town.

5. Write a stream-of-consciousness story about a third baseman at work.

Caught in a Draft

Where do major league teams find new players? Before the free agent draft began in 1965, teams competed with each other to sign the best young prospects. They learned about these prospects from reports submitted by their scouts. Some teams with big budgets had dozens of scouts traveling all over the country, watching high school and college teams play and keeping track of the best players. A New York Yankees scout working in Oklahoma discovered Mickey Mantle when Mickey was just sixteen years old. Teams paid full-time scouts a regular salary and part-time scouts only when one of their discoveries signed a contract. The part-timers were called "bird dogs."

The free agent draft was created to make the selection of young players fairer for teams that could not afford a large scouting staff. Now the team with the worst won-lost record at the end of the season makes the first pick in the free agent draft held the following spring. The Major League Scouting Bureau collects reports from scouts around the country and makes them available to all teams before the draft takes place.

All scouts use strict guidelines to evaluate players. No matter which team a scout works for, the guidelines are the same. Pitchers are judged on how fast they can throw, their control, and any other pitches they may use besides the fastball, such as curves, sliders, or knuckleballs. Non-pitchers are judged on their running speed, throwing ability, fielding, hitting, and hitting for power. Scouts also try to predict how a player's abilities will develop as he grows and evaluate all players for poise, aggressiveness, and baseball instincts. These attributes are harder to measure, but an experienced scout is usually able to recognize them, even in a young player. A scout once said, "What you really want to know about a young player is how much stomach does he have." The scout was referring to courage and determination, sometimes called "guts."

Scouts are human and can make mistakes. Many "can't miss" prospects were drafted first and never made it out of the minors. Then there is the story of Dodgers catcher Mike Piazza, one of the outstanding players in the game today. Mike was drafted in the sixty-second round of the 1988 free agent draft, after more than thirteen hundred players had been selected. In 1993, his first year in the majors, he won the National League Rookie of the Year Award. Mike Piazza is proof of how difficult and frustrating a scout's job can be.

From *Reading Baseball*, published by Good Year Books. Copyright © 1997 Barbara Gregorich and Christopher Jennison.

From *Reading Baseball*, published by Good Year Books. Copyright © 1997 Barbara Gregorich and Christopher Jennison.

NAME _____   DATE _____

PROJECTS

1. Write a poem about a Little Leaguer being watched by a bird dog.

2. Imagine that you are the first baseball scout ever. You want to develop a scouting chart (report) that you can use while watching a game. Invent such a chart.

3. In the 1989 draft, six players were chosen before the White Sox got to choose.

1 - Orioles chose pitcher Ben McDonald;
2 - Braves chose catcher Tyler Houston;
3 - Mariners chose pitcher Roger Salkeld;
4 - Phillies chose outfielder Jeff Jackson;
5 - Rangers chose outfielder Donald Harris;
6 - Cardinals chose outfielder Paul Coleman.

Do some research to learn about these other players and to learn who the Sox chose. Then write a "Memo to Our Scouts" from the general manager of one of the first six teams. What might the GM say to the scouts two or three years after the choices were made?

4. How important is diet to athletic performance? What do major league baseball players eat? Do major league teams employ team dietitians? Do some library and/or interview work to discover the answers to these questions. Then write a report on the subject.

5. Do more major leaguers come from one area of the country than from another? Get the current roster of one major league team. Then use a book such as *Total Baseball* (New York: Viking, 1995) or *The Baseball Encyclopedia* (New York: Macmillan, 1996) to learn where these players were born. Make a chart showing the geographic origins (states where they were born) of every player on the roster.

Hooray for Hoy!

Born in Ohio during the Civil War, William Ellsworth Hoy spent eighteen years playing professional baseball: four years in the minor leagues, fourteen in the majors. His lifetime batting average was .287. This speedy center fielder stole a league-leading eighty-two bases for the Washington Senators in 1888, his first year in the majors. In 1891 he used his keen sense of sight to draw a league-leading 119 walks. In 1901, when he was thirty-nine years old and near the end of his career, he again led the league in walks. But Hoy is best remembered for something else.

William Ellsworth Hoy was born able to hear, but spinal meningitis left him deaf by the age of two years old. In those days, a deaf person was called "Dummy." Hoy is listed in baseball records as Dummy Hoy. He was never ashamed of the name.

Although he graduated from the Ohio School for the Deaf and became a shoemaker, Hoy secretly longed to be a major league ballplayer. But in addition to being deaf, he was short, standing only 5'4" tall. Still, he left his job and home and traveled to Wisconsin to play in the minor leagues in 1885.

Hoy hit only .219 his first year in professional baseball. At that time, umpires called balls and strikes only by speaking. To understand what the umpire had said, Hoy had to turn around and read the umpire's lips. As soon as Hoy turned around, the opposing pitcher threw again, before Hoy had a chance to get settled in the batter's box.

In addition to having a keen eye, fast feet, great courage, and a strong desire to succeed, Hoy was also an intelligent and innovative problem solver. He asked his third base coach to signal him whether the pitch was a ball or a strike. After the coach started to relay the signals, Hoy's batting average skyrocketed. In 1887 he batted .367 and helped his team win the pennant.

Almost immediately baseball umpires, coaches, managers, and players recognized that hand signals for *ball, strike, safe, out, fair,* and *foul* were in many cases superior to voice signals. Umpires adopted the new signals and use them to this day. Because of William Hoy, whether you can hear the umpire or not, you can understand the call if you can see the hand signals.

Dummy Hoy was a very popular player. Some of his teammates even learned sign language so they could communicate with him. And the fans? The fans, knowing that Hoy couldn't hear their clapping, fans gave him a visual sign. Whenever he made a great play, they would stand and with great enthusiasm wave their arms and hats in the air. It meant, "Hooray! Great play! We appreciate you!

From *Reading Baseball*, published by Good Year Books. Copyright © 1997 Barbara Gregorich and Christopher Jennison.

PROjecTs

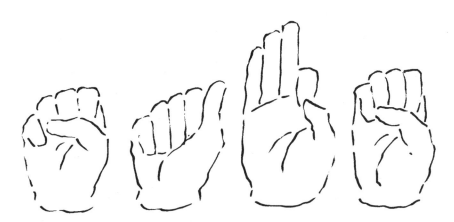

From *Reading Baseball*, published by Good Year Books. Copyright © 1997 Barbara Gregorich and Christopher Jennison.

1. Find magazine or newspaper articles in the library about Curtis Pride, a deaf ballplayer with the Detroit Tigers organization. Write your own newspaper article about Pride.

2. Learn about the hand signals that umpires use. Draw a chart showing each hand signal and what it means.

3. Others have played major league ball despite physical handicaps or challenges — Mordecai Brown, Bo Jackson, and John Olerud, for example. Read about these three players and write a medical report on each one's physical handicap or challenge and how it affected his baseball career.

4. Write a poem about William Hoy.

5. Imagine a day in your life with no sound. Write a description of what your life would be like during that day.

Instruction

The coach has taught her
how to swing,
run bases, slide,
how to throw
to second,
flip off her mask for fouls.

Now, on her own, she studies
how to knock the dirt out of her cleats,
hitch up her pants, miss her shoulder
with a stream of spit, bump
her fist into her catcher's mitt,
and stare incredulously at the ump.

—Conrad Hilberry

Used by permission of the author.

From *Reading Baseball*, published by Good Year Books. Copyright © 1997 Barbara Gregorich and Christopher Jennison.

PROjecTs

1. There are two levels of "instruction" going on in the poem. What are the two levels, and who is doing the instruction in each level? Write an explanation of what the poem means.

2. Photos of baseball players often show their attitude toward something that is happening. Collect such photos from newspapers or magazines. Cut them out and make a collage out of them. If you want to, title your collage.

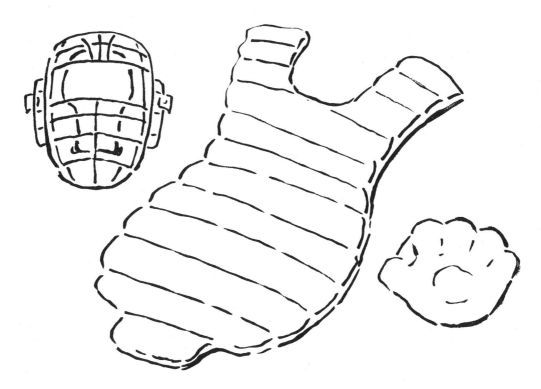

3. Imagine the mother or father of the catcher in the poem. What do they think of their daughter's behavior? Write a letter from one of the parents to an advice columnist. Then write the columnist's reply.

4. Create a *Behavior Dictionary for Ballplayers*. Think up at least a dozen words to define. You can choose nouns such as *dirt* or *pants*. Or you can choose verbs such as *spit* and *stare*. Define each word in terms of how a ballplayer is supposed to behave.

5. What do catchers and umpires say to one another behind home plate? Write a dialogue between a catcher and an umpire for half an inning.

Big: As in Unit, as in Hurt

The many similarities between Randy Johnson and Frank Thomas start with the obvious: that they are both professional baseball players. Both play in the American League, Johnson for the Seattle Mariners, Thomas for the Chicago White Sox. Both are big men. At 6'10", Johnson towers over others. Put that height on an already-elevated pitcher's mound, and you have a Seattle Space Needle glaring down at you. At 6'5", Thomas is no shorty. Weighing in at 240 pounds, he stands at the plate like the Sears Tower. Impressive. Formidable. Both men dominate their league, Johnson as a pitcher, Thomas as a hitter. And both have nicknames given them by fellow players looking up at (and to) them. Randy Johnson is the "Big Unit," Frank Thomas is the "Big Hurt."

The differences between these players are less a matter of the physical than the mental. When Randy Johnson came up to the major leagues, he had blazing speed, striking out eight, nine, ten batters a game. He also had little control, walking three, four, five, six batters a game, congesting the base paths with opponent runners. After he had been in the majors for five years, Johnson received some helpful pitching advice from Nolan Ryan and Tom House. As a result, the Big Unit's control improved dramatically. He walked only half the number of batters he once walked. He also struck out even more batters than

before. In 1995 the Big Unit struck out 12.35 batters per nine innings, a new major league record.

Frank Thomas came to the major leagues with power and control. In his first full season, he led the league in walks, drawing 138 of them. His keen eye and strict discipline, which kept Thomas from swinging at pitches outside the strike zone, gave him an on-base-percentage of .454 that year: a league-leading number. Most impressive about the Big Hurt is the way he combines power and control to hit. In each of his first four seasons, Thomas batted .300 or better, hit 20 homers or more, batted in 100 runs or more, scored 100 runs or more, and drew 100 walks or more. Only two other players in history have done that for four consecutive seasons: Ted Williams and Lou Gehrig. In 1995 Thomas accomplished the same thing for a fifth year in a row.

From *Reading Baseball*, published by Good Year Books. Copyright © 1997 Barbara Gregorich and Christopher Jennison.

PROJECTS

1. Baseball players acquire nicknames in many different ways. Thomas and Johnson got their nicknames from a physical characteristic: size. Think about what nicknames might refer to, then list five possible categories that might inspire nicknames. Using baseball reference books, find five examples of nicknames from each category. Use at least one example from the Negro Leagues and one from the All-American Girls Baseball League in each of the five categories.

2. Write the lyrics to a song about either the Big Unit or the Big Hurt.

3. In 1994, when Frank Thomas faced the possibility of equaling Williams and Gehrig in the five offense categories of batting average, homers, runs-batted-in, walks, and runs scored, almost all reporters overlooked the one player who had achieved these numbers for six consecutive seasons. That player was Ted Williams. Read about Williams to discover what was unique about his career that causes reporters to overlook his six-consecutive-seasons record. Prepare a speech on Williams and his record.

4. Do some deep statistical research at a library, in a newspaper, or through a baseball statistics service to learn what Frank Thomas's stats against Randy Johnson are. When the Big Hurt faces the Big Unit, what are the results?

5. Figurative language is colorful language that does not mean exactly what the words say, as in Randy Johnson is "a Seattle Space Needle glaring down at you." Four types of figurative language are *metaphor, simile, hyperbole,* and *personification.* Look up the meaning of each of these four terms and write a definition of it. Then write two colorful examples of each type of figurative language, describing a baseball player of your choice.

THE LONG SEARCH

Let me put it this way: the job wasn't easy. There were times I thought I'd never find it. Times I felt like a baseball scout, looking for that one-in-a-million prospect—only I'm not a baseball scout, I'm a private eye. Cody's the name, detecting's the game.

I thought I'd found it down in a Texas college town, where the weather was hot and the baseball was not. Great view. Trouble was, the thing was in that buzzard sun all day long. No shade. Sun about set my cap on fire. Northward in Nebraska, I detected bleachers covered by a simple roof. Shelter from the sun, shelter from the rain, a nice breeze blowing. I could see the pitcher, the catcher, the batter, the umpire's signals. Best of all, I was in a position to catch home runs. Yeah.

But face it, even a private eye needs support. Back up. Things got to the point where I couldn't sit in another backless bleacher seat if my life depended on it. The grapevine told me of a stadium in Washington State where the bleachers had backs.

Never trust the grapevine. Sure, the bleachers had backs, little short back rests, just below the shoulders. The view was great, but the small of my back was killing me. So I figured, lose the minor league towns, Cody, lose the bleachers, and find the big leagues.

Chicago called me like a catcher calling pitches. Wrigley Field. The ivy on the walls was beautiful. I sat in the upper deck. Just past first base. Oh, those Cubbie-blue seats felt good. Comfortable seats that supported me everywhere, know what I mean? This is it, I thought. I've found it! But then . . . then I looked toward home plate, and what did I see?

A post, that's what. A beam. A metal support. An obstruction! I tell you, those old ballparks are beautiful, but the posts are not. As long as I was in the City of the Big Shoulders, though, I thought I'd look for it in Comiskey Park. New Comiskey, that is. They tore the old one down a few years ago. Took away all the obstructions.

After a climb that would exhaust a mountain goat, I sat there in the upper deck, looking down at the players. Way, way down. Cody, I said, you still haven't found it. What kind of detective are you?

So I investigated one more major league city, one more team. Yeah, Cody found it. The seat supports are high-grade aluminum, the body high-density polyethylene, and the thing is ergonomically designed, with a curved seat and a back that really supports. Sturdy arm rests, seat twenty-two inches wide. I see the rise of the pitcher's mound, watch the shortstop at work head-on, see and hear every runner pounding down to first. I catch the outfield action, too. It's perfect, man, perfect. And I'm the one who found it.

What? You want to know where it is?

Get real.

pRojecTs

1. Choose a subject that seems to have nothing to do with detectives and write a private-eye parody.

2. Imagine that you have been hired by a major league baseball club to write a brochure describing the various types of seats in the stadium. The purpose of the brochure is to get fans to buy season tickets. Write such a brochure.

3. Write a scene in which two friends are trying to decide where to sit at a baseball game. One is interested in what can be seen from the seat, while the other is interested in the physical characteristics of the seat itself.

4. For marketing purposes, fiction is divided into *genres,* or types. Mystery is one genre, romance another, westerns a third, and techno-thrillers a fourth. Within mysteries is a subgenre of private-eye novels, and within that subgenre is a small category of private-eye novels in which the detective was at one time a baseball player, either high school, college, minor league, or major league. Of all the sports that fictional private eyes have participated in or follow, baseball outnumbers the others by far. Why are more private eyes former baseball players than football players, basketball players, hockey players, or such? Think about this question, then write a well-thought-out answer to it.

5. Read John Keats's poem "Ode on a Grecian Urn." Then write a one-stanza parody of the poem entitled "Ode on a Stadium Seat."

Native American Players

Professional baseball started with the Cincinnati Reds in 1869. Native Americans began to play the game professionally just a few years later.

Louis Sockalexis was a Penobscot Indian from Maine, born in 1871 and raised on a reservation. He attended school and played baseball. Louis's father was upset that his son played a "white man's game," but Louis kept on playing. Sockalexis attended Notre Dame University, then signed with the Cleveland American League team in 1897. A powerful left-handed hitter, he once won a game by blasting a home run in the tenth inning. Fans shouted "Sock it to them, Sockalexis."

Three other Native Americans in baseball were Charles Albert Bender, John Tortes Meyers, and Allie Reynolds. The non-Indian ballplayers called each of these men "Chief," as they did every Native American out of disrespect and ignorance.

An Ojibwa from Minnesota, Charles Albert Bender attended Carlisle Indian School, where he pitched. From 1903 to 1914 he pitched for the Philadelphia Athletics, twice winning more than twenty games (1910 and 1913). Bender pitched in five World Series, compiling a 6–4 record.

John Tortes Meyers was a catcher, he played for the Giants from 1909 to 1915, then for the Dodgers and the Boston Braves. He finished his baseball career in 1917 with a lifetime batting average of .291.

Allie Pierce Reynolds, a Creek Indian from Oklahoma, graduated from Oklahoma State University. From 1942 to 1946 he pitched for the Cleveland Indians, and from 1947 to 1954, for the Yankees. A right hander, he compiled a 182–107 record. In 1952 he racked up twenty wins, his 2.06 ERA leading the American League. Reynolds hurled two no-hitters, both of them in 1951.

Bob Bennett is a Native American in organized baseball today. A Lakota Sioux, he's related to the great Sioux leader Crazy Horse. Bennett attended Dartmouth College, where he minored in Native American studies. In 1994 he played with the minor league Modesto A's in California. A pitcher, he wears his hair in a braid. When he goes to the mound, he says a prayer and sprinkles a bit of tobacco on the ground as an offering. "The tobacco is a gift to the spirits," he explains.

Bob Bennett's teammates don't call him Chief. A reporter asked him what he thinks of team nicknames such as "Braves" and "Redskins." Bennett replied, "I don't like it, but I don't get all fired up about it, either. I'm an Indian, and I'm proud of it. When I see people doing the [tomahawk] chop or wearing warpaint, I just shake my head."

From *Reading Baseball*, published by Good Year Books. Copyright © 1997 Barbara Gregorich and Christopher Jennison.

pRojecTs

1. Imagine that you are a Native American ballplayer. How are you treated by the non-Indian ballplayers? Write a "Memo to Myself" about what you see and hear, and how you react to it.

2. Choose one of the Indian groups mentioned in the article. Read about its customs and culture. Draw maps showing the tribe's original home and current location. Write a report on the group.

3. Write a pro or con "Letter to the Editor" about sports teams with names such as "Braves," "Indians," and "Redskins."

4. In 1950 sports reporters voted Jim Thorpe the greatest male athlete of the first half of the twentieth century and Babe Didrikson the greatest female athlete of that same period. Read about Jim Thorpe. Make a list of at least twenty facts about Thorpe, highlighting each fact in the list with a bullet (•). At the end of the list, write a one-paragraph conclusion that expresses your opinion about Thorpe.

DEAR EDITOR,
I LIKED THE ARTICLE ON BASEBALL FANS, AND THE THINGS THEY DO, BUT I THINK THE ATLANTA TOMAHAWK CHOP IS INSULTING TO NATIVE AMERICANS.

5. What if Native Americans had succeeded in defending their lands against westward-moving settlers over the last several hundred years? How would things in North America be different? Write a fictional story about the situation.

Letter of Resignation

In 1921 baseball owners created the position of baseball commissioner. They asked federal judge Kenesaw Mountain Landis to take the position for life. His job was to maintain the integrity of the game of baseball. After Landis died, owners made the post of baseball commissioner last for a term, not for life. On September 7, 1992, Baseball Commissioner Francis "Fay" Vincent sent a letter of resignation to the owners.

To: American and National League Owners

As requested in the owners' resolution of September 3, 1992, . . . I tender my resignation as Commissioner of Baseball, effective immediately.

On August 20, I wrote each of the owners I would not resign the Office of the Commissioner of Baseball. I stated that, in my judgment, to do so would be a great disservice to the Office of the Commissioner and to baseball itself. I strongly believe a Baseball Commissioner should serve a full term. . . . Only then can difficult decisions be made impartially and without fear of political repercussion. Unfortunately, some want the Commissioner to put aside the responsibility to act in the "best interests of baseball"; some want the Commissioner to represent only owners, and to do their bidding in all matters. I haven't done that, and I could not do so, because I accepted the position believing the Commissioner has a higher duty. . . .

Unique power was granted to the Commissioner of Baseball for sound reasons—to maintain the integrity of the game and to temper owner decisions predicated solely on self-interest. . . . My views on this have not changed. What has changed, however, is my opinion that it would be an even greater disservice to baseball if I were to precipitate a protracted fight over the Office of Commissioner. . . .

I cannot govern as Commissioner without the consent of owners to be governed. I do not believe that consent is now available to me. Simply put, I've concluded that resignation—not litigation—should be my final act as Commissioner "in the best interests" of baseball.

I can only hope that owners will realize that a strong Commissioner . . . is integral to baseball. I hope they learn this lesson before too much damage is done to the game, to the players, umpires and others who work in the game, and most importantly, to the fans. . . .

Sincerely,
Francis T. Vincent, Jr.

From *Reading Baseball*, published by Good Year Books. Copyright © 1997 Barbara Gregorich and Christopher Jennison.

pRojecTs

1. What is *integrity?* Read the dictionary definition of it, then write an essay explaining what integrity is. Be sure to use examples to illustrate your point.

2. Write a want ad that begins with the headline "Wanted: Baseball Commissioner."

3. Read about Judge Kenesaw Mountain Landis as baseball commissioner. Write a list of five important decisions he made as commissioner. After each decision, write your opinion of the decision.

4. Do some research in magazines and newspapers to find out why Fay Vincent resigned.

5. Imagine that citizens get to vote for baseball commissioner every four years. Choose any two public figures (they can be athletes, politicians, lawyers, or whatever you choose) who might run for the office. Write a campaign speech for each.

From Hand To Heart

Baseball's Golden Age: The Photography of Charles M. Conlon, by Neal McCabe and Constance McCabe, published by Harry N. Abrams, Inc., 1993. 205 black-and-white photographs.

The cover is a black-and-white photo of a masculine hand gripping a baseball. The hand is large, with dirt embedded in the knuckles and under the fingernails. The hair follicles are visible, as are the strong veins. The grip is that of a pitcher; the ball nestling in the curve formed by the index finger and thumb. The ball itself is scuffed and stained, but still more white than black.

Today's pristine white baseballs, Astroturf, and synthetic fabrics are light-years removed from what this photo tells us about the game of baseball. The photo predates even radio broadcasts, reminding us that baseball used to be played on real grass, and only the fans present at the time witnessed the victories and losses.

The hand belongs to Chicago White Sox pitcher Ed Walsh, who went on to the Hall of Fame. The greatest hurler of the dead ball era, Walsh once won forty games in a season. His lifetime ERA of 1.82 is a major league record. Charles M. Conlon, the greatest baseball photographer who ever lived, took the photo around 1913. A shy proofreader, Conlon photographed the national pastime out of love from 1904 to 1942. The choice of this photo for the cover of *Baseball's Golden Age* signals the alert reader that something big is happening here—not just to Big Ed Walsh, who is demonstrating how to throw the spitball, but to the photographer, to the authors, and to us, the perusers of this book. What does this photo evoke if not Jim Bouton's poignant observation: "You spend a good piece of your life gripping a baseball and in the end it turns out that it was the other way around all the time."

Baseball gripped the heart of every player and manager pictured in the book; it gripped the heart of Conlon; it must have gripped the hearts of Neal and Constance McCabe, the brother-and-sister team who produced this book; and it will grip the reader's heart, too, through the depth and clarity of Conlon's photographs.

To choose the 205 pictures arranged in this book, the McCabes went through eight thousand original Conlon negatives. Neal McCabe arranged the photos in the order we see them, and Constance McCabe printed them from the original negatives. The pictures speak to us across the years. The captions identify, elucidate, and tantalize, and, like the photographs, help us see. This is a book no baseball fan should be without.

PROJECTS

1. Find this book in a library. Take a lot of time to go through the book, looking at photos and reading captions. Then write your own book report.

2. Choose any black-and-white photo of a ballplayer from the period before 1950 and any color photo of a ballplayer from today. Give a speech in which you compare and contrast the two photos.

3. Imagine that all of a sudden publishers decide to print books in which all old black-and-white photographs, like the ones Conlon took, are colorized. Movie studios who sell their classic black-and-white films to video packagers have already allowed many old black-and-white movies to be colorized. What do you think of colorizing black-and-white photos or movies? Write a letter to the manager of a publishing company on the subject.

4. Locate baseball photos in *Sports Illustrated.* Analyze how each photographer creates a mood or feeling through the photo. Pick two of the photos and describe how they make you feel.

5. Write a scene from a play about Conlon trying to take photographs of today's baseball players.

From *Reading Baseball*, published by Good Year Books. Copyright © 1997 Barbara Gregorich and Christopher Jennison.

Haiku for The Seasons

Summer

Ace begins the eighth
God's midday fastball steals his
Looking for relief

Autumn

The game's chilly war
Lardner called it "serious"
Fall will come for one

—Mark Schraf

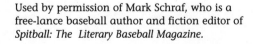

Used by permission of Mark Schraf, who is a
free-lance baseball author and fiction editor of
Spitball: The Literary Baseball Magazine.

pRojecTs

1. Read about haiku. Write a paper on the subject. Be certain to give the history of haiku, explain what a haiku is, and discuss some of the best-known writers of haiku.

2. These haiku focus on two seasons. Write one baseball haiku titled "Spring" and another titled "Winter."

3. Imagine that you are the team trainer in "Summer." What kinds of things would you have the pitcher do to keep from losing his fastball in the midday sun?

4. In literature, an *allusion* is a reference to a famous event, real or mythical. Mark Schraf alludes to something when he writes, "Lardner called it 'serious.'" Be a historical detective: do some research to discover what Schraf is alluding to. Give a speech on the subject.

5. Baseball begins in February, with spring training, and ends in October with the World Series. What do baseball players do during the winter? Imagine that you're a professional ballplayer and it's winter. Write a friendly letter to another ballplayer, telling what you're doing during the winter and what your thoughts are for the coming season.

THE BOX SCORE

Angels 6, Indians 5											
Cleveland	AB	R	H	BI	Avg.	California	AB	R	H	BI	Avg.
Amaro cf	3	0	0	0	.147	Phillips 3b	5	1	3	1	.290
Vizquel ss	4	0	1	1	.263	Edmonds cf	4	0	1	1	.308
Baerga 2b	4	0	1	0	.326	Salmon rf	3	0	0	1	.301
Belle lf	5	1	1	0	.302	CDavis dh	2	1	0	0	.343
MRamirez rf	4	1	0	0	.326	Snow 1b	4	1	1	0	.324
Thome 3b	5	2	2	1	.331	GAnderson lf	4	1	2	2	.338
HPerry 1b	3	0	1	2	.348	Easley 2b	1	1	0	1	.199
Srrnto 1b	2	0	1	0	.257	Myers c	4	0	0	0	.244
Winfield dh	2	1	1	0	.174	Fabregas c	0	0	0	0	.281
SAlomar c	3	0	2	1	.386	DiSarcina ss	3	1	2	0	.316
TOTALS	26	6	10	5		TOTALS	23	6	8	6	

Cleveland	012 001 100 —	5 10 0
California	122 100 00x —	6 9 0

WP - Finley (9–7) **LP** - Hershiser (7–5) **Umpires** — Home, Ford; First, Young; Second, Reilly; Third, Garcia. T- 3:23 A- 42,468

In most newspapers the box score takes up a space approximately 1.5 inches by 2.5 inches. The extra information usually provided at the bottom of the box (not duplicated here) almost doubles the space taken. Even so, the space occupied is minimal, and the amount of information packed into it is huge.

It first it reveals that the Angels defeated the Indians, 6–5. Because Cleveland is listed on the left-hand side and California on the right, the reader knows that the game took place in California, with the opponents batting first. The names of the players are printed in their batting order, or lineup, with each player's position abbreviated after the name.

Amaro, the center fielder, batted first for Cleveland, followed by Vizquel, the shortstop, and Baerga, the second baseman. Belle, the left fielder, batted cleanup, or fourth. In the case of Ramirez, Perry, Alomar, Davis, and Anderson, a first initial is given as well as a last name: this indicates that other current major league players have the same last name.

Both teams used pinch hitters or substitutes at some point in the game: Sorrento for Perry at first base and Fabregas for Myers as catcher. Also, as American League teams, both the Indians and Angels use a designated hitter (dh) who bats for the pitcher.

Continued on page 100

From *Reading Baseball*, published by Good Year Books. Copyright © 1997 Barbara Gregorich and Christopher Jennison.

The Box Score

The abbreviations across the top of the lineup stand for at bats, runs scored, hits, runs batted in, and batting average. You can see that Angels third baseman Phillips had five at-bats and collected three hits. He scored one run and batted in one run. When the game ended, his batting average for the year was .290.

Toward the bottom of the box, the inning-by-inning score is given. By the bottom of the first inning the Angels were leading, 1–0. By the bottom of the third, they were leading, 5–3. Notice that the Angels, the home team, did not bat in the bottom of the ninth. They weren't required to bat because the score was 6–5 in their favor going into the top of the ninth, and when the Indians failed to score then, the Angels won. Three numbers follow the inning-by-inning score: 5–10–0 for Cleveland and 6–9–0 for California. These always stand for runs-hits-errors. Cleveland scored five runs on ten hits and committed no errors. California scored six runs on nine hits and committed no errors.

At the very bottom of this box score, you can see that the winning pitcher was Finley, whose won-loss record became 9–7 at the end of the game. The losing pitcher was Hershiser, whose record became 7–5. The four umpires and the positions they covered are listed next. The *T* stands for time, or how long the game took. And the *A* stands for attendance—42,468 fans paid to see the game. The next morning, millions more read about it in the box score.

From *Reading Baseball*, published by Good Year Books. Copyright © 1997 Barbara Gregorich and Christopher Jennison.

pRojecTs

1. Choose any box score from any newspaper, as long as it contains all the additional information missing from the box score in this activity. Write an article explaining all the other information and what it means.

2. Imagine that it is the year 3000, and somewhere out in space people from another civilization find a time capsule from the United States. Everything in the time capsule has disintegrated except for three box scores. Write a science fiction story in which the people from the other civilization try to interpret the meaning of the box scores.

3. Have you always suspected that you are perfect, but that your friends and family are not? Here is your chance to show it. Compose a box score of two teams made up of you and your family and friends. These are National League teams, so the pitcher—that's you—must come to bat. You throw a perfect game: twenty-seven batters face you and you retire each and every one of them. Write the box score for this magnificent performance.

4. Go to a library to research the history of the box score. Write a report telling who invented it, when, and why. How has the box score changed over the years?

5. What do you think of the length of major league baseball games today? Imagine that you are the editor of a school newspaper. Write an editorial on the length of major league games.

From *Reading Baseball*, published by Good Year Books. Copyright © 1997 Barbara Gregorich and Christopher Jennison.

The Atlanta Braves

Although the Braves have resided in Atlanta only since 1966, theirs is the second-oldest franchise in baseball, exceeded in age only by the Chicago Cubs. Unlike the Cubs, whose history is intertwined with that of Chicago, the Braves have called three distinctly different cities home.

Professional baseball originated in 1869 in Cincinnati, when the Red Stockings of that city started to play for pay. When the Cincinnati team decided to return to amateur status, star Harry Wright and three of his teammates moved to Boston, forming the Boston Red Stockings in 1871. The Atlanta Braves are direct descendants of this team. Because Wright and his teammates were exceptionally good ballplayers, Boston won four pennants in five years. By the late eighties (that's the 1880s!) the team was called the Boston Beaneaters. From 1890–1902, the Beaneaters won five National League pennants. Center fielder Hugh Duffy batted .440 in 1894—a major league record. The Beaneaters of that year scored 1,221 runs—also a major league record.

After 1902 the Beaneaters sank in the standings, once losing 108 games in a season. While they managed precious few victories, they did acquire a new nickname: the Braves. Perhaps this helped, for in 1914 the Braves had the kind of year that lives in legend. The team was in the cellar of an eight-team league by mid-July. One week later, after winning six straight games, the team rose to third place. One month later, the Braves were in second place. By the end of August, they were in first place! The Boston Braves won the National League pennant by ten and a half games! In the World Series, they faced the heavily favored Philadelphia Athletics. The Boston Braves swept the A's and won their first modern-era world championship.

The following year, the Braves finished second, then went into a thirty-year slump. In 1946 they woke up with the pitching of Warren Spahn and Johnny Sain. Two years later, they won the pennant, but lost the World Series to Cleveland. Fan interest tapered off, and in 1953 the owner moved the franchise to Milwaukee,

Continued on page 104

From *Reading Baseball*, published by Good Year Books. Copyright © 1997 Barbara Gregorich and Christopher Jennison.

The Atlanta Braves

where the team retained its nickname as the Milwaukee Braves. With the addition of slugging third baseman Eddie Mathews and "Hammerin' Hank" Aaron, the Braves were going places. They won the 1957 pennant and then defeated the Yankees in seven games to become world champions. In 1958 the team won the pennant again but lost the World Series. Attendance slowly dropped, and at the end of the 1965 season, the franchise moved again, this time to Atlanta.

Ted Turner bought the Braves in 1976 and began to build them into powerful contenders. The Atlanta Braves won division titles in the 1980s, but lost the League Championship Series (LCS). Finishing last in 1990, the Braves won their division in 1991: the first time a National League team has moved from the bottom to the top in consecutive years. With the addition of Ron

Gant and Dave Justice and with formidable pitchers Tom Glavine, Steve Avery, and John Smolz, the Braves looked unstoppable. Winning the LCS, the 1991 Braves faced the Minnesota Twins in the World Series, losing to them in seven games—in what many fans say was the most exciting World Series ever played. In 1992 the Braves again won the division and the pennant, but lost the Series to the Toronto Blue Jays in six games. With the addition of pitcher Greg Maddux in 1993, Atlanta won the division but lost the playoffs to the Pittsburgh Pirates.

In 1995 the Atlanta Braves faced the Cleveland Indians in the World Series. The Indians had last won the Series in 1948, when they defeated the Boston Braves, four games to two. In 1995 history reversed itself, and the Atlanta Braves—at long last—won the World Series, four games to two.

From *Reading Baseball*, published by Good Year Books. Copyright © 1997 Barbara Gregorich and Christopher Jennison.

NAME _____   DATE _____

pROjecTs

1. At the library, find books on nineteenth-century baseball or on the history of baseball. Read about Hugh Duffy. Prepare a speech on Duffy.

2. Do some on-line research about the Cleveland and Atlanta teams. Access their World Wide Web pages if they have them. Read what their on-line fans have to say. Download some of the material you find and print it out. Give a report on your findings.

3. Read about Boston, Milwaukee, and Atlanta. Make a chart comparing the three cities. Show history, population, tourist attractions, weather, etc.

4. Read Henry Aaron's autobiography and write a book review of it.

5. Imagine that it is the year 2020, and the Braves have moved back to Boston. Write an advertisement for the Braves in a Boston newspaper.

The Curse of the Billy Goat

SETTING: Wrigley Field, Chicago, May 1994. As the curtain rises, fans outside Wrigley crowd the turnstiles. There is much crowd noise, some music.

MALE FAN #1: Are the Cubbies gonna win today?

TICKET TAKER *(young woman dressed in blue uniform):* I hope so. *(She tears his ticket and gives him the stub.)*

MALE FAN #1: I hope not! If they lose today, they'll set a record! It will be the Cubbies' longest losing streak of the twentieth century!

TICKET TAKER *(frowning):* Next, please.

DANTE *(Young man holding a long blue canvas cargo bag in his arms. A home-made Cubs logo has been stitched onto the cargo bag. It is obvious that the package is heavy.):* Don't worry, the Cubs won't lose today.

TICKET TAKER: I hope not. *(She notices his large bundle, frowns.)* Ticket, please.

DANTE: Uh, it's here, in my fingers. *(Nods with his head, to indicate that he's holding the ticket but can't hand it to her because of the cargo bag.)*

TICKET TAKER *(takes ticket, inspects it carefully):* I have to ask you what's in the package. You can't bring beverages into the ballpark.

DANTE: It's not a beverage.

MALE FAN #2: Peanuts! Hey, guys, get a load of this. The guy in front of me is tryin' to sneak a cargo bag fulla peanuts into Wrigley Field! He must expect the Cubs to lose big! *(Laughter from fans.)*

FEMALE FAN #1: It's not peanuts, you bozo. Peanuts don't move.

PACKAGE: Baaaa!

TICKET TAKER: What was that?

DANTE: Uh, nothing. I was clearing my throat. Can I go through now?

TICKET TAKER: No. Please open the package so I can see what it contains.

DANTE: Look, I promise it's not beer. Or soft drinks. Nothing like that. It's nothing that will hurt anybody. In fact, it'll help the Cubs win.

TICKET TAKER *(firmly):* Open the package or I'll call Security.

Continued on page 108

From *Reading Baseball*, published by Good Year Books. Copyright © 1997 Barbara Gregorich and Christopher Jennison.

The Curse of the Billy Goat

FEMALE FAN #1 *(listening intently to package and petting it):* It's a goat! He's bringing a billy goat to the game!

PACKAGE: Baaaa!

TICKET TAKER: Step aside, please, so others can get through. Open the package.

DANTE steps aside, opens package. GOAT stands up, shakes itself, looks around.

FANS: Hey! A goat! The guy's bringing a billy goat! Hooray! Let's hear it for the billy goat!

TICKET TAKER *(sternly):* You know our policy on goats, sir. We've made it very clear over the years.

DANTE: Don't you see? That's the problem! There's been a curse on the Cubs ever since 1945, when "Billy Goat" Sianis bought two tickets to the Cubs *vs.* Tigers World Series. One for him and one for his pet goat, Sonovia.

TICKET TAKER: So you do know our policy on goats.

DANTE: The Cubs turned away Sianis and his goat. You don't want to make the same mistake, do you?

MALE FAN #2: Yeah, old Billy Goat Sianis put a hex on the Cubs, saying they'd never be in another World Series until they let the goat onto the field. Let the goat in!

DANTE: That's right. My goat is a direct descendant of Sonovia.

GOAT: Baaaa!

FANS: Let the goat in!

TICKET TAKER *(sadly):* We aren't going to be in the World Series this year.

DANTE: We will be if you let the goat in. It will lift the curse! The Cubs will win.

FANS: Let the goat in! Let the goat in! Cubs will win! Cubs will win!

GOAT: Baaaa!

pRojecTs

1. Imagine that a new owner has purchased the Chicago Cubs. She feels that the Cubbies have an image problem. She proposes to change this image by changing the team's nickname to the Chicago Grizzlies. What kind of pro and con arguments over this proposal might you hear around the management conference table? Write a video script for such a scene.

2. Read about goats. Write a report on goats, including their natural history, their care and temperament, the ways in which humans raise them, and historical myths associated with goats.

3. Hold a class audition for actors for this scene. While the actors are rehearsing, the rest of the class should write another scene from this play. Then the cast should rehearse both scenes and put on a show.

4. Study the team histories of both the Atlanta Braves and the Detroit Tigers in this book. Then write a team history of the Chicago Cubs.

5. Some teams, such as the Phillies and the Blue Jays, have mascots. Others, such as the Chicago Cubs, do not. Imagine that the Cubs have decided on a mascot. Imagine that you have been hired to play the role. Write a journal entry of your first day inside the mascot's costume.

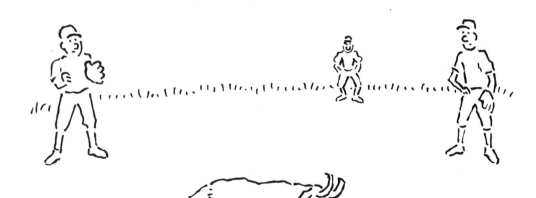

From *Reading Baseball*, published by Good Year Books. Copyright © 1997 Barbara Gregorich and Christopher Jennison.

The Gift of Beisu Boru

Just as it is difficult to pinpoint the exact origins of baseball in the United States, so is it difficult to pinpoint its exact introduction to Japan. But historians agree that *beisu boru,* as it's called, was introduced to Japan during the 1870s, probably by an American professor. Perhaps he knew the value of the gift he gave, perhaps not.

The game spread rapidly throughout Japanese colleges. By the first decade of the twentieth century, American college teams sailed to Japan to play against the local college teams. In 1913 the major leagues visited Japan in the form of the Chicago White Sox and the New York Giants, who were on a world tour. During the 1920s many more major league teams, All-Star teams, and individual players visited Japan to play *beisu boru.*

In the United States, baseball no longer reigns in popularity as it once did. Football and basketball rival it in attracting fans. But baseball is still the most pervasive sport in America—its history goes back the longest, its vocabulary enlivens our language, and hundreds of baseball books fill the shelves of bookstores, libraries, and homes. In Japan, *sumo* used to be the most popular sport, but *beisu boru* replaced it. Today Japanese professional baseball teams draw more fans per game than do American major league teams. And in Japan there are more newspapers devoted to the game than there are in the U.S.

Just as American baseball overflows with tales of heroism and excellence—of individuals striving against the odds and winning—so too does *beisu boru.* There's Eiji Sawamura, a mere high school student who during a 1934 game faced U.S. sluggers Charlie Gehringer, Babe Ruth, Lou Gehrig, and Jimmie Foxx all in a row, and whiffed them.

There's Shigeo Nagashima, who played for the Yomiuri Giants from 1958–1974. "Mr. Giant" led the league in home runs and RBIs his rookie year. One year later, his team played in front of the emperor and empress of Japan. Nagashima won the game with a home run in the ninth inning. On the day he retired,

Continued on page 112

From *Reading Baseball,* published by Good Year Books. Copyright © 1997 Barbara Gregorich and Christopher Jennison.

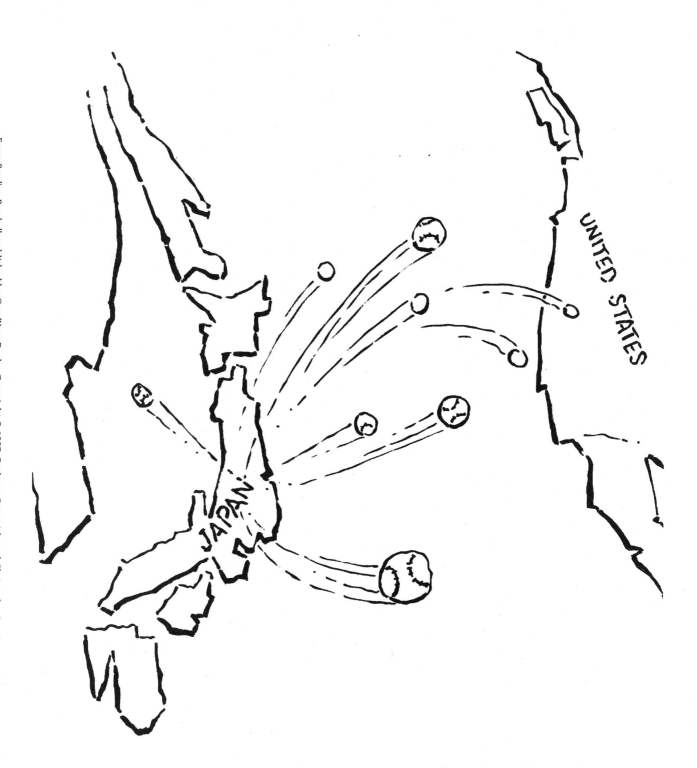

UNITED STATES

JAPAN

The Gift of Beisu Boru

Nagashima hit his 444th home run, then, with tears in his eyes, said goodbye to his fans, who begged him not to retire.

And there's Sudaharu Oh, teammate of Nagashima. Oh hit more homers than any player in history: more than Babe Ruth, more than Hank Aaron. His record of 868 home runs just might stand forever.

Today scores of U.S. major leaguers sign contracts with Japanese teams. Cecil Fielder, slugger for the Detroit Tigers, played in Japan before returning to American baseball. Julio Franco left the Chicago White Sox to play in Japan.

But the baseball exchange is starting to move in the other direction. Until 1995 American major league teams had signed only one Japanese player: Masanori Murakami, who pitched for the San Francisco Giants in 1964 and 1965 before returning to Japan. But in 1995 the Los Angeles Dodgers signed Hideo Nomo, a young pitcher known for whiffing Japanese batters left and right. Facing U.S. batters, Nomo continued his great success and became wildly popular in the bargain, both here and in Japan. The gift given to Japan more than a century ago has come back as a gift to the United States.

From *Reading Baseball*, published by Good Year Books. Copyright © 1997 Barbara Gregorich and Christopher Jennison.

PROjecTs

1. View the movie *Mr. Baseball* starring Tom Selleck. Write a movie review of the film, answering some of these questions: Who is the hero? What does he want? What stands in his way? How does the hero change by the end of the film?

2. The Japanese method of baseball training differs greatly from the American method. At a library, research the subject in books and periodicals. Write a report comparing and contrasting the two different methods of training.

3. Imagine that sumo wrestling, introduced to the United States by the Japanese, somehow becomes the most popular sport in the country, surpassing football, basketball, baseball, and hockey. Write a letter to a friend in England, explaining how sumo's popularity has affected American culture.

4. Write a haiku about Hideo Nomo.

5. "The best gift is one that comes back to you." Write several paragraphs explaining this statement. Agree or disagree with it. Give examples of what you mean.

Answer Key

From *Reading Baseball*, published by GoodYear Books. Copyright © 1997 Barbara Gregorich and Christopher Jennison.

Roberto Clemente
1. F
2. O
3. O
4. F
5. F
6. F
7. Answers will vary.
8. Answers will vary.

As He Sees Them
A. 3, 1, 2
B. 1, 2, 3
C. 2, 3, 1
D. 2, 3, 1; or 3, 2, 1
E. Answers will vary.
F. Answers will vary.

Take Me Out to the Ball Game
1. He wants to go to Coney Island (Isle).
2. Coney Island is in New York City.
3. Jack Norworth
4. "Take me out to the ball game"
5. Nelly Kelly
6. ev'ry (also—they'd; let's)
7. three; two
8. Answers will vary.

Rickey Henderson
1. F
2. T
3. T
4. F
5. F
6. F

7. T
8. T
9. F
10. T

Letters to the Editor
1. J. T. Smith
2. Joe Average Citizen; Melissa
3. Melissa
4. Joe Average Citizen
5. Melissa
6. J. T. Smith
7. Melissa
8. Joe Average Citizen
9. Answers will vary.

How to Play First Base
1. you want to give the pitcher a good target.
2. the ball reaches your glove faster and the runner is out sooner.
3. playing one-handed will make you a swifter, surer fielder.
4. runners can take extra bases and even score.
5. it allows you to field the ball as soon as possible.
6. it increases your chance of fielding the ball and preventing the run. You want to guard the foul line.
7. you want to help the catcher get the runner out. You want to alert the catcher that the runner is trying to steal second.
8. you want to give the outfielder a good target to throw to.

Answer Key

The Secret Life of Bats
1. transport
2. inspire
3. jinx
4. midst
5. discard
6. speckled
7. defect
8. fussy
9. convince
10. fashion
11. affection
12. superstition

The Negro Leagues Book
1. 242
2. 51
3. 381
4. 371
5. 11
6. 159
7. 255
8. 33
9. 15
10. 167

It's a Hit
1. *A* is not the best summary because the article is not about score keeping.
2. *C* is not the best summary because it emphasizes the batter's reaction time.
3. *B* is the best summary because it says the same thing the article says, in the same order.

Overdog
1. fan
2. underdog
3. creams it
4. batter
5. smokes it
6. athletes for whom everything is easy
7. Ho-hum.
8. Answers will vary.
9. Illustrations will vary.

A League of Their Own
1. Yes
2. No
3. No
4. Yes
5. Yes
6. Yes
7. Yes
8. No
9. Yes
10. Yes
11. Answers will vary.

What If?
Answers will vary.

From *Reading Baseball*, published by Good Year Books. Copyright © 1997 Barbara Gregorich and Christopher Jennison.

Answer Key

From *Reading Baseball*, published by Good Year Books. Copyright © 1997 Barbara Gregorich and Christopher Jennison.

Rabid Fans

A. Answers will vary.
B. Answers will vary.
C. Answers will vary.
1. b
2. g
3. f
4. a
5. c
6. d

Slants, Whiffs, and Safeties
Answers will vary.

Visualize Yourself

1. Mitch will pitch well and prevent the opponents from scoring.
2. Tyler will hit the ball and drive in the runners.
3. Charles will drop the ball.
4. A fireman is a relief pitcher who keeps the hot opponent fire from spreading; a fireman keeps the opponents from scoring.
5. A cleanup hitter clears the bases by hitting a home run or at least hitting for extra bases to drive in runs. The fourth batter in the lineup bats cleanup.
6. A goat is a player who makes a major mistake that costs the team the game.
7. Answers will vary.

Interview with Nellie M. Kearns

1. It means that the outfielder must really run after the ball.
2. It means that she was so tired she couldn't stay on her toes, as a fielder should to be ready to move immediately. Instead, she stood flat, on her heels.
3. They probably assumed that because they were men, they would easily defeat a team of women.
4. a) The Rangers played on ill-kept fields.
   b) The Rangers did not have trainers on hand to take care of injured players.
   c) The Rangers played as many games a day as they could get.
   d) The Rangers traveled every where because they did not belong to a league.
   e) Every day the Rangers went out exploring the new towns they visited.
   Other answers may apply.
5. Answers will vary.

The Baseball

1. First Stanza: space, race
   Second Stanza: flight, sight
   Third Stanza: command, hand
2. It gives the feeling of the ball coming down and the poem ending. It gives a feeling of completion or success.

Answer Key

3. A ball rises and falls in a curved way. The poet might be trying to re-create the path of the ball's flight.
4. rise, space, rocket, hovers, peak, flight, dives, air's, landing
5. Poems will vary.

Baseball's Treasure Trove
1. painstakingly
2. trove
3. genealogist
4. raze
5. diagnose
6. dissertation
7. donate
8. anticipation

1. a) Christy Mathewson's piano
   b) Casey Stengel's baby picture
   c) a cloth blueprint of the original Comiskey Park
   d) Lou Gehrig's letter to his wife
2. Answers will vary.

Pride Goeth
A is the most accurate summary because it says the same thing the article says, in the same order.
Answers will vary.

Classic vs. Modern

Griffith	*SkyDome*
classic	modern
1911	1989
388	328
320	328
421 and 408	400
Many sides and angles	Symmetrical, oval-like shape
City streets, university, lumber mill	City streets, expressway

Classic	*Modern*
Answers will vary.	Answers will vary.
Early twentieth century	1950–1990s
Walk, public transportation	Cars, sometimes public transportation

Answers will vary.

Martin Dihigo
1. His batting average improves.
2. He is elected to the Baseball Hall of Fame in three countries.
3. He is not signed to play in the major leagues.
4. Dihigo is a great hitter.
5. He is tall and agile, with tremendous range to his left and right.
6. Sports reporters write only about white baseball players.
7. Dihigo is outstanding at hitting, pitching, and fielding.

From *Reading Baseball*, published by Good Year Books. Copyright © 1997 Barbara Gregorich and Christopher Jennison.

Answer Key

How to Be a Person First

1. a) Went to Peaches games
   b) Collected Peaches autographs
   c) Went to fan picnics
   d) Kept a Peaches scrapbook
   Answers will vary.
2. a) Took her Peaches souvenirs wherever she went
   b) Remembered the heroes of her youth
   c) Decided to interview surviving Peaches players
   Answers will vary.
3. She wrote a book about the Peaches.
4. Snookie grew up playing sports and believing she could be whatever she wanted to be.
5. Susan grew up believing that you can succeed at doing what you love and are good at whether you're a boy or a girl.
6. Answers will vary.

Humongous Trivia

1. d
2. f
3. h
4. b
5. i
6. a
7. g
8. c

1. Chris
2. from books or newspapers, possibly from an on-line source
3. The average length is a lot fewer than thirteen letters—perhaps six, seven, or eight. In the United States, it is unusual to have a last name that is thirteen letters long.
4. He likes baseball; he likes his best friend Mac; he gets a bit impatient with trivia, but he's willing to participate in order to please his friend; he has a sense of humor; he believes he can achieve his goals.
   Answers will vary.
5. He will become the first major leaguer to have a last name longer than thirteen letters.